katie lee's easy-breezy eats

katie lee's
easy-breezy eats
the endless summer cookbook

Katie Lee

photography by lucy schaeffer

ABRAMS, NEW YORK

"And so with the sunshine and the great bursts of leaves growing on the trees, just as things grow in fast movies,

I had that familiar conviction that life was beginning over again with the summer"

— F. Scott Fitzgerald, *The Great Gatsby*

contents

light meals 40

cornbread panzanella 44

green gazpacho 47

chilled beet soup with
yogurt and pepitas 48

grilled chicken paillard with
arugula and shaved pecorino 50

salmon salad with lemon dijon
caper vinaigrette 51

soba noodle salad 52

spinach salad with pickled
strawberries and poppyseed
dressing 53

kale caesar salad 54

croutons 55

kale pesto 55

vietnamese beef and noodle
salad bowls 57

salade niçoise 58

chinese chicken salad 60

thai cod cakes 62

grilled escarole salad
with citrus 63

late summer farro, butternut squash,
and arugula salad 65

lentil salad 66

grilled zucchini, corn, black bean,
and avocado salad 67

lobster reubens 68

burgers, tacos + pizza 70

blt ranch burgers 74

shrimp burgers with
old bay mayo 78

turkey burgers with caramelized
onions, cheddar, and peach
chipotle ketchup 79

italian sausage and pepper
burgers 80

steak tacos with pickled radishes
and mashed avocados 84

adobo chicken tacos with
pico de gallo and grilled corn 85

grilled smoky tofu tacos with
black beans, peach cucumber
salsa, and lime sour cream 86

fish tacos with creamy chipotle
sauce and pico de gallo 88

una pizza napoletana 90

pizza dough 93

grilled pizza 94

cocktail hour

dinner

sides 156

desserts 184

introduction

The other day, I came across this quote from Henry James:

> *"Summer afternoon—summer afternoon; to me those have always been the two most beautiful words in the English language."*

It's so simple and put so perfectly. When I read it, that feeling of a summer afternoon was instantly evoked—a warm breeze, the sun high in the sky, reading a novel under the shade of a wide-brimmed hat and biting into a juicy peach, and the feeling of trying to hold my eyes open but then just giving in to a nap. Or long lunches with a group of friends, wine, laughter, and no attention paid to time whatsoever.

For me, there is no greater place to be in the summer than the Hamptons. The area is special all year long, but summer is my ultimate. I count the days from Labor Day to Memorial Day, anxiously awaiting the summer sun. About six years ago, I started surfing and everything changed for me. I used to be afraid of the ocean; I would only go in the water to my knees. The inspiration hit during a difficult time in my life—I had gone to the beach to clear my mind (as I so often do), and I watched the surfers riding waves. They looked so free. I wanted to feel that way. I left, went straight to a local surf shop, bought a wetsuit, and signed up for a lesson. It was one of the best moves I've ever made. Surfing allowed me a deeper connection to nature, a place of peace, and a way to let go. I also found that everything tastes better after surfing. I dream of an endless summer.

Many people hear "The Hamptons" and a certain image comes to mind—the glitz, glamour, fancy parties, paparazzi, playground of the rich and famous—well, yes, but not exactly. Before I moved here, I didn't know much of the area except from what I had seen on an awful made-for-television documentary called *The Hamptons*, which followed a group of wealthy, mostly obnoxious people who lived up to all of the stereotypes of the rich and powerful. I thought it looked like a pretty unappealing place to be, to put it mildly. As fate would have it, I ended up falling in love with someone who not only called the Hamptons home, but who also appeared on that very namesake series. As a girl from a small town in West Virginia, I did not know what I was getting myself into when I packed my bags and headed north. I think I half expected to get mowed over by a drunken blonde in a Mercedes SUV or to be mistaken as "the staff" at one of those swank parties where I no more belonged than I would in a hardcore biker gang. What I found upon my arrival was much more Green Acres than Park Avenue, and though at times I did feel a bit like a Beverly Hillbilly, I quickly became comfortable, like *this must be the place where I am meant to be.*

Twelve years later, my love for this little sliver of land known as the South Fork only continues to grow. It amazes me that just a mere ninety miles from New York City exists this bucolic community of farmers, artists, writers, and surfers set on farm fields and quite possibly the most beautiful beaches in the world. There is sun, pristine water, and food so fresh it bites *you*. The rich and fertile soil combined with the salty sea breezes produces the ripest tomatoes, the sweetest corn, and the crispiest lettuce. From the sea, striped bass, fluke, tuna, crab, scallops, oysters, and more. We have chicken farms, dairy farms, and artisanal cheese makers. Vineyards dot the landscape generating impressive, esoteric wines. Though it can feel as if you've taken a step back in time as you cross the Shinnecock Canal, the juxtaposition of country life to modern day affluence certainly exists. Tell me, where else in the world can you see a tractor puttering down an oceanfront road, a potato farm to one side and a multi-million dollar home to the other, while holding up a Ferrari in traffic?

All those over-used buzzwords like "seasonal" and "local" are not the latest food fad here, but a way of life, as in my childhood home in West Virginia. I grew up in a tight-knit family that centered our days around our meals, talking about the next day's breakfast at dinner, lunch at breakfast, and so on. My grandfather was a true green thumb and had an expansive garden that yielded all of our vegetables, his cousin raised cows, another cousin raised pigs,

introduction

and everyone made a practice of sharing their crops. I came to the Hamptons expecting to feel like an outsider, and instead I found life to be concurrent with my upbringing. Just like at home, people here were eating farm-to-table well before it was called "farm-to-table."

I am all about comfort food but to be truly comforted by food, I need to know where it came from and how it got to my plate. I like knowing the story of my food; it tastes better that way. The area has greatly influenced my cooking style, though not in the traditional sense of adapting foods from a particular region. While we do have the greatest ingredients available, there is not a particular cuisine or even a dish that is indigenous to the Hamptons. It's not like Texas and barbecue, or New Orleans and po' boys, or Alabama and biscuits. Maybe this is because of the large WASP population in the early days, people who would rather drink gin and tonics than sit down to a feast. Instead, I think it is those aforementioned parties that are native to this neck of the woods. But at my house, the parties are anything but fancy, much more low-key. I like to keep it casual, comfortable, and chic. I entertain often and I joke that my house practically has a revolving door of guests coming to visit. Friends come by for casual lunches, sunset cocktails, barbecues, and themed dinners. Nothing is better than surfing all day, stopping at the farm stand for food, cooking, and sharing a meal with loved ones.

Some of my favorite meals have been those that I have planned the least. Like the time a fisherman friend dropped off a large striped bass he had just caught as a thank you for a long-forgotten favor. I set off for the farm stand, picked up tomatoes, peppers, corn, and peaches, and made fish tacos with grilled corn and peach salsa for a group of hungry friends who had assembled upon hearing news of said taco dinner. The absolute best is when I pull up to the Green Thumb, run by the same family since the 1600s, and Mrs. Halsey tells me she has fresh eggs. Once you have had one of these eggs, there is no going back to supermarket eggs. The yolk is a deep, dark orange, perfect with just a sprinkling of flaky sea salt and a dash of pepper, sopped up with buttered toast. I will take those eggs home like they are a gift of gold and whip them up for my sleepy houseguests who have just roused from their beds.

In this book, I share with you my healthy, farm fresh, easy recipes. I want you to know the Hamptons the way I know it, the spirit of this magical place, the beauty of what it truly is. I hope this book motivates you to not only cook these recipes, but also to connect with your surroundings the way I have with mine and to seek out the treasures that lie within your own community.

Remember, perfection is not the goal—it is about creating a relaxed environment where everyone feels welcome.

morning

fuel

Breakfast is one of two things for me: grab-and-go fuel for sustenance before I go surfing or do a kick-butt workout, or a leisurely "Let's prolong the start of the day so we don't really have to get anything accomplished" type of meal. I'm fine with the former, but if I have my druthers, I prefer the latter. My friends and I call this kind of breakfast "cawfee tawk," and we sit around and gossip, pontificate, and beat the events of the prior night to death. I put on an extra-large pot of coffee and make a simple breakfast. I have no interest in being a short-order cook—I want to be part of the fun!

My friend Marcy Blum is the queen of cawfee tawk. Marcy is an event planner extraordinaire, and boy does she have interesting insights on just about everything. I'll wake up before she does and bang around the kitchen trying to make enough noise to "accidentally" wake her from slumber. It is always the same routine: I hear her schlump down the stairs, she walks into the kitchen, hair in every direction and last night's mascara under her eyes, and she says, "What's wrong with you people, why are you so awake and chipper?" Then she proceeds to make everyone laugh with her ever-witty commentary. Marcy, this chapter's for you.

nectarine and cream cheese french toast sandwiches MAKES 4 SANDWICHES

Stone fruits are at their peak in July and August. I am constantly stopping at a favorite farm stand, the Green Thumb, to pick up peaches, plums, apricots, and nectarines. Most often, I enjoy them immediately, leaning over the kitchen sink, juice dripping off my chin as I sink my teeth into their sweet flesh, but occasionally they make it to the next morning and find their way into a French toast sandwich.

3 tablespoons salted butter

2 nectarines, cut in half, pits removed, and thinly sliced

8 (¼-inch/6-mm) slices challah or brioche

6 tablespoons (85 g) cream cheese

4 large eggs

¼ cup (60 ml) milk

2 tablespoons granulated sugar

1 teaspoon vanilla extract

Confectioners' sugar

In a small skillet, melt 1 tablespoon of the butter over medium heat. Add the nectarines and cook for 4 to 5 minutes, until softened. Remove from the heat.

Spread each slice of bread with cream cheese. Divide the nectarines evenly among four slices of bread and top with the remaining bread to build sandwiches.

In a shallow dish, whisk the eggs, milk, sugar, and vanilla together. Carefully dip the sandwiches into the egg mixture and turn to coat.

Melt the remaining 2 tablespoons butter on a griddle over medium heat. Cook the sandwiches for 2 to 3 minutes per side, until golden brown. Dust with confectioners' sugar and serve.

ricotta cheese works too!

grilled doughnuts with melted nutella

MAKES 4 DOUGHNUTS

It's pretty darn difficult to improve on a doughnut, but if they've sat around one day too long and you need to breathe some life back into them, just pop them in a panini press. In just a few minutes, they'll be warm and crunchy on the outside and tender inside.

4   cinnamon sugar doughnuts

¼   cup (60 g) Nutella

Preheat a panini press to medium-high. Place the doughnuts inside and cook for 2 to 3 minutes. (If you don't have a panini press, you can use a grill pan and place a weight on top of the doughnuts to press them down.) Meanwhile, microwave the Nutella until melted, about 40 seconds. While the doughnuts are still warm, use a spoon to drizzle melted Nutella over the tops. Serve the doughnuts with the Nutella for dipping.

grilled doughnuts with ricotta and honey MAKES 4 DOUGHNUTS

4   yeast doughnuts

¼   cup (60 g) ricotta cheese

1   tablespoon honey

Preheat a panini press to medium-high. Place the doughnuts inside and cook for 2 to 3 minutes. (If you don't have a panini press, you can use a grill pan and place a weight on top of the doughnuts to press them down.) Meanwhile, whisk the ricotta and honey in a small bowl. Serve with the doughnuts as a spread.

breakfast bread MAKES 4 PIECES

Breakfast bread is kind of like a pizza with eggs on it. Like 99.9 percent of the population, I like shortcuts in the morning, so I make this using store-bought naan (an Indian bread) instead of making homemade. Everything goes right on the naan and gets baked to perfection. I like the eggs kind of runny, so that when you cut into the bread the yolk oozes out and creates a rich sauce as it mixes with the hot ricotta and melted Gruyère.

1	(8.8-ounce/246-g) package (4 pieces) naan bread (I like Stonefire brand)
½	cup (120 g) ricotta
4	eggs
	Flaky sea salt (I like Maldon) and freshly ground black pepper
8	slices prosciutto
	Handful of cherry tomatoes, halved
½	cup (60 g) grated Gruyère cheese
2	scallions, white and light green parts only, thinly sliced

Preheat the oven to 400°F (205°C). Spray a baking sheet with nonstick cooking spray.

Spread 2 tablespoons of the ricotta evenly onto each naan. Carefully crack the eggs onto the ricotta, 1 egg per naan. Sprinkle with sea salt and pepper. Place 2 slices of prosciutto around each egg, scatter with the tomatoes, and top with the Gruyère and scallions.

Bake until the eggs are set, 10 to 15 minutes, depending on how well you like to cook your egg yolks. Serve hot.

huevos rancheros SERVES 4

I first started making these a couple of years ago when I had houseguests. I was up early piddling around while everyone else was still sleeping (as per usual), and I wanted to cook something different for breakfast. I had just bought these new individual baking dishes and was itching to use them, so I made up this recipe for huevos rancheros. It was a hit and quickly became part of my repertoire.

Olive oil

1 onion, diced

1 red bell pepper, cored and diced

1 serrano chile, diced

2 cloves garlic, minced

1 teaspoon dried oregano

1 (28-ounce/793-g) can crushed tomatoes

1 (15-ounce/425-g) can black beans, drained and rinsed

¼ cup (25 g) chopped fresh cilantro, plus more for garnish

8 eggs

1 cup (120 g) grated Monterey Jack–cheddar cheese blend

Sour cream

Guacamole

Preheat the oven to 350°F (175°C).

In a medium skillet, heat the oil over medium heat. Add the onion and sauté until tender, about 5 to 7 minutes. Add the bell pepper, then the chile. Add the garlic. Stir in the oregano, tomatoes, and beans and bring to a simmer, about 5 minutes. Reduce the heat, cover, and cook for 10 minutes. Add the ¼ cup cilantro and stir.

Ladle into 4 individual-serving-size baking dishes. Crack 2 eggs into each dish and sprinkle with the cheese. Bake for 15 minutes, or until the eggs are set to your liking. Sprinkle with cilantro and serve hot with sour cream and guacamole.

triple coconut waffles MAKES 8 WAFFLES

Coconut is all the rage in healthy eating, and luckily it tastes good too. I make these waffles with coconut milk, coconut oil, and shredded coconut for a triple threat. They are yummy for breakfast, but save some so you have leftovers to serve later for dessert with vanilla ice cream and a little hot fudge.

2	large eggs, separated
½	cup (120 ml) coconut oil, melted and cooled
2	cups (480 ml) light coconut milk
1 ⅔	cup (200 g) white spelt or all-purpose flour
¼	cup (25 g) unsweetened shredded coconut
⅓	cup (45 g) cornstarch
2	teaspoons baking powder
½	teaspoon salt
2	tablespoons sugar
	Maple syrup

Preheat a waffle iron.

In a medium bowl, whisk the egg yolks with the oil to create an emulsion. Whisk in the coconut milk.

In another bowl, whisk together the flour, coconut, cornstarch, baking powder, and salt. Add to the egg mixture and stir until combined.

Using a handheld electric mixer, in a third bowl, whisk the egg whites with the sugar until firm soft peaks form.

Gently fold the egg whites into the batter until just combined; do not overmix.

Working in batches, make waffles in the waffle iron according to the manufacturer's instructions. (I use about ½ cup/120 ml batter for each waffle and cook them for about 4 minutes.) To keep your waffles warm until serving time, place them on a baking sheet in an oven preheated to 200°F (100°C) as they are made. Serve hot with maple syrup.

smoothies

Smoothie time! A few years ago I invested in a Vitamix blender. I love the thing. I make smoothies quite often, and I love to pack them with flavorful, healthy ingredients. These are a few of my go-to combinations. You can follow the recipes exactly, or adapt them to your taste.

yellow smoothie

MAKES ABOUT 4 CUPS (960 ML); SERVES 2

2   ripe bananas

1   cup (165 g) frozen-mango chunks

½   cup (120 ml) plain or vanilla low-fat yogurt

2   tablespoons honey

2   teaspoons flax seeds

1   teaspoon ground turmeric

½   teaspoon ground ginger

Put the bananas, mango, yogurt, honey, flax seeds, turmeric, and ginger in a blender and puree until smooth. Serve immediately.

green smoothie

MAKES ABOUT 3 CUPS (720 ML); SERVES 2

1   Granny Smith apple, cored and coarsely chopped

2   kiwi fruit, peeled and coarsely chopped

1   cup (30 g) packed baby spinach leaves

1   cup (240 ml) unsweetened almond milk

½   cup (120 ml) plain low-fat yogurt

1   tablespoon honey

1   teaspoon matcha (fine green tea) powder

Put the apple, kiwi, spinach, almond milk, yogurt, honey, and matcha powder in a blender and puree until smooth. Serve immediately.

red smoothie

MAKES ABOUT 3 ½ CUPS (840 ML); SERVES 2

2   cups (300 g) frozen strawberries

1   cup (140 g) frozen raspberries

1   cup (240 ml) plain low-fat yogurt

1   cup (240 ml) unsweetened almond milk

1   tablespoon chia seeds

1   teaspoon honey

Put the strawberries, raspberries, yogurt, almond milk, chia seeds, and honey in a blender and puree until very smooth. Serve immediately.

strawberry kiwi quinoa breakfast parfait SERVES 4

These breakfast parfaits look so pretty and colorful and are so tasty, you'd never know they're also super healthy. The Greek yogurt is packed with protein, the quinoa is also high in protein and has double the amount of fiber of most grains, and the strawberries and kiwi are both high in vitamin C and antioxidants. What a way to start the day!

2 cups (480 ml) plain Greek yogurt (I use 2%, but you can use any kind you like)

1 tablespoon honey

Finely grated zest of ½ lime

1 cup (185 g) cooked quinoa, cooled

8 large strawberries, diced

2 kiwi fruit, peeled and diced

In a small bowl, whisk together the yogurt, honey, and lime zest.

Place 4 small (6-ounce/180-ml) juice glasses on a work surface and put 2 tablespoons of the quinoa in the bottom of each glass. Add ¼ cup (60 ml) of the yogurt to each glass, followed by about 2 tablespoons of the diced strawberries and kiwi. Repeat the layering in each glass, and scatter any additional fruit that is left over the top layer of yogurt. Serve immediately.

rolled shrimp, goat cheese, and dill omelet SERVES 4

On *The Kitchen*, I do a regular segment called "Leftover L'Oven," where I take leftovers and transform them into a totally new dish. I like to think of it as giving leftovers a "makeover," kind of like on those morning shows when they pluck an unsuspecting woman from the crowd, do her hair, put makeup on her, and—poof— she suddenly has a new look. In this recipe, I was inspired by leftover shrimp cocktail. The next day, I don't really want to eat shrimp cocktail straight from the fridge. So why not put it in an omelet? And in order to avoid making individual omelets for everyone in the house, why not make one big omelet?

8	large eggs
½	cup (120 ml) whole milk
¼	cup (30 g) all-purpose flour
2	teaspoons dry ground mustard powder
	Finely grated zest of 1 lemon
¼	cup (25 g) chopped fresh dill, plus more for garnish
	Salt and freshly ground black pepper
6	ounces (170 g) chopped cooked shrimp (about 1 ½ cups)
2	ounces (55 g) feta or fresh goat cheese, crumbled

Preheat the oven to 350°F (175°C). Brush a high-sided jellyroll pan (10 ½ by 15 ½ inches/26.5 by 39 cm) with vegetable oil. Line the pan with parchment paper, cutting the paper larger than the pan so that it hangs over the pan edges by at least 1 inch (2.5 cm).

In a large bowl, whisk the eggs until blended. In a small bowl, whisk the milk, flour, mustard, and lemon zest until smooth; whisk into the eggs. Add the dill, season well with salt and pepper, and whisk until combined. Pour into the prepared pan.

Evenly scatter the shrimp and cheese over the top of the egg mixture. Bake until the eggs are completely set, 18 to 20 minutes. Remove from the oven and let stand for a couple of minutes.

Starting at one of the shorter ends, roll up the omelet, peeling back the parchment paper. Lift the omelet out of the pan and transfer it to a large cutting board or serving platter. Cut the omelet into ½-inch (12-mm) slices, garnish each with a sprinkling of dill, and serve warm or at room temperature.

chilaquiles frittata SERVES 8

Chilaquiles is a traditional Mexican dish made from corn tortillas that are cut into strips, fried, and then simmered in salsa. They are often eaten for breakfast with eggs. One morning I found myself blankly staring at the pantry (if it had been a cartoon, there would have been a cloud above my head with a great big question mark), and then it hit me: a bag of slightly stale tortilla chips. Eureka! (Question mark now changes to lightbulb in the imaginary cartoon.) I'll make a frittata with the chips to shortcut my way to a chilaquiles breakfast. (While eating, all my guests' bubbles revealed an exclamation point!)

10	large eggs
2	cups (170 g) crushed tortilla chips
¼	cup (25 g) chopped fresh cilantro
¼	teaspoon salt
¼	teaspoon freshly ground black pepper
1	tablespoon olive oil
8	scallions, white parts only, thinly sliced
1	serrano chile, minced
1	cup (180 g) chopped tomatoes
1	cup (165 g) corn kernels (cut from the cob or thawed if frozen)
1	(4-ounce/113-g) can diced green chiles
1	cup (120 g) grated Monterey Jack–cheddar cheese blend
	Sour cream
	Salsa

Preheat the oven to 300°F (150°C).

In a large bowl, whisk the eggs. Add the tortilla chips, cilantro, salt, and pepper. Set aside.

Heat the oil in a large ovenproof nonstick skillet over medium-high heat. Add the scallions and serrano chile and sauté until softened, about 2 minutes. Add the tomatoes, corn, and green chiles and cook for about 3 minutes, until the corn is cooked through and the tomatoes have softened. Pour the egg mixture into the pan and top with the cheese.

Transfer to the oven and bake for 20 minutes, or until lightly browned and fluffy. (Note that the temperature is low, and this recipe cooks longer than a typical frittata; I find that cooking eggs low and slow results in better flavor and texture.) Cut into wedges and serve with sour cream and salsa.

healthy banana oat muffins

MAKES 12 MUFFINS

I like to start the day off healthy with muffins like these. I much prefer spelt flour to whole-wheat flour when baking, as it can be substituted cup-for-cup for regular all-purpose flour. You can feel good about all of the ingredients in these muffins. In the fall, try using mashed pumpkin instead of banana for a different spin.

2	cups (240 g) spelt flour
2	teaspoons baking powder
½	teaspoon baking soda
1	teaspoon ground cinnamon
¾	teaspoon salt
⅓	cup (27 g) rolled oats, plus 2 tablespoons for sprinkling
1	cup (260 g) mashed ripe bananas (about 3 bananas)
1½	teaspoons fresh lemon juice
½	cup (120 ml) plain Greek yogurt (I use 2%, but you can use full-fat if you like)
2	large eggs, lightly beaten
½	cup (120 ml) maple syrup
¼	cup (60 ml) coconut oil, melted and cooled
2	teaspoons vanilla extract

Preheat the oven to 350°F (175°C). Place paper liners in a 12-cup muffin pan and spray with nonstick cooking spray.

Sift the flour, baking powder, baking soda, cinnamon, and salt into a medium bowl. Stir in the oats.

In a large bowl, whisk the bananas, lemon juice, yogurt, eggs, maple syrup, coconut oil, and vanilla together. Stir in the dry ingredients and mix until just combined; do not overmix! Use an ice cream scoop to evenly distribute the batter into the prepared pan. Sprinkle the tops with oats.

Bake for about 25 minutes, until the tops are golden brown and a toothpick inserted in the center of a muffin comes out clean. Let cool on a wire rack for a few minutes before removing from the tin.

blender pancakes

MAKES 4–6 MEDIUM-SIZED PANCAKES

You will never look at pancakes the same way again. It truly doesn't get any easier than this. Pancakes on a weekday before work or getting the kids off to school? No problem! They can be done in about five minutes. They are healthy, full of fiber and protein, and you can give them more of a boost by adding some flax seeds or chia seeds. I've found that if I use Greek yogurt instead of cottage cheese, I sometimes need to add a tiny splash of milk to the batter; yogurt will also make for a slightly denser, more protein-rich pancake.

1   **cup (240 ml) cottage cheese or Greek yogurt**

2   **large eggs**

1   **cup (80 g) rolled oats**

Preheat a griddle over medium-high heat.

Put the cottage cheese, eggs, and oats in a blender and blend until smooth.

Spray the griddle with nonstick cooking spray. Pour the batter from the blender onto the griddle to make your desired size of pancakes. Cook until bubbles start to form on the surface of the pancakes about 1 to 1 ½ minutes. Flip and cook for 1 minute more. Serve with maple syrup, butter, jam, whatever you like!

serve with maple syrup,
butter, jam, whatever you like!

light
meals

My most memorable lunch happened by chance. A friend invited me to go paddleboarding on Sagg Pond in Sagaponack. Sagg Pond is a unique body of water—it's sort of a salt pond, and on the southernmost end it butts up against Sagg Main Beach. Sometimes the strip of sand opens up—forming what's called a "let"—and the water flows between the ocean and the pond. Almost all of the land surrounding the pond is private estates, and the best way to see the houses is by hopping in the water with a paddleboard or a kayak.

Aside from getting a good look at how the one percent of the one percent live, Sagg Pond is also an excellent location for crabbing. That day we thought we'd try for a few blue crabs to bring home and make a little lunch if we were lucky. (And yes, Southampton Town Police, I have a shellfish license.)

We placed an old plastic milk crate on the tip of the board, tied a raw chicken leg to a string, and set out. Let me tell you, crabs love raw chicken legs. That day we had more crabs on that chicken leg than I had ever seen. Using our nets, we scooped them up by the dozen, put them in the milk crate, and turned right back around and headed home. I texted some friends to come over for lunch.

As soon as I got home, I put a pot of water on the stove to boil, loaded it up with Old Bay seasoning, covered the outdoor picnic table in old newspapers, and blended up mayo with Sriracha while the crabs steamed. We opened (several) bottles of a local rosé and spent the rest of the afternoon cracking open the crabs, scooping out little bits of the sweet meat, and laughing until our faces hurt. It was pure summer magic.

cornbread panzanella serves 4-6

Every evening my grandma used to make a fresh loaf of cornbread. It would come out of the oven hot and crunchy on the outside and moist on the inside. Panzanella is a dish that I had maybe made once or twice in the past, but I must have gotten a wild hair one day and decided to try making it with cornbread instead of a crusty white bread—it was my way of "southernizing" the recipe. I loved it. Panzanella is so bright and colorful—it just looks like summer.

For the salad:

Olive oil

1 loaf cornbread, cut into 1-inch (2.5 cm) cubes

Salt

1 red bell pepper, cored and chopped

1 yellow bell pepper, cored and chopped

1 English cucumber, chopped

1 pint (10 ounces/280 g) grape tomatoes, halved

½ red onion, thinly sliced

15 fresh basil leaves, torn

For the dressing:

1 tablespoon Dijon mustard

¼ cup (60 ml) red wine vinegar

½ cup (120 ml) extra-virgin olive oil

2 tablespoons chopped capers

½ teaspoon salt

¼ teaspoon freshly ground black pepper

Make the salad: Preheat the oven to 400°F (205°C). Oil a baking sheet.

Put the cornbread on the prepared baking sheet, drizzle with oil, and season with salt. Bake until nicely toasted, about 15 minutes. Let cool completely.

In a large salad bowl, combine the cornbread, peppers, cucumber, tomatoes, onion, and basil.

Make the dressing: In a small bowl, whisk all the ingredients together.

Add the dressing to the cornbread and vegetables and toss. Let stand at room temperature for about 20 minutes before serving.

green gazpacho

*chilled beet soup
with yogurt + pepitas*

green gazpacho SERVES 6-8

A chilled soup on a hot day is so refreshing. The farm stands have a selection of the most beautiful heirloom tomatoes when in season. One day, I thought the Green Zebras looked cool, so I bought a bunch of them, not knowing quite what I'd do with them. They served as a pretty centerpiece in a big wooden bowl on my counter until I figured it out: gazpacho. The avocado in this recipe adds an extra element of creaminess, and the lime juice evens out the flavors of the onion, garlic, and jalapeño. If I am serving it for an outdoor meal on a hot day, I like to stick the bowls in the freezer for a few minutes before ladling in the soup so it stays nice and cold.

2	pounds (910 g) Green Zebra tomatoes, cored and coarsely chopped, plus 1 Green Zebra tomato, cut into small wedges, for garnish
1	unpeeled seedless cucumber, coarsely chopped, plus 1 finely diced unpeeled cucumber for garnish
1	sweet onion, coarsely chopped
1	Hass avocado, chopped
1	small jalapeño, seeded
1	clove garlic
2	tablespoons fresh lime juice
2	tablespoons fresh mint leaves, chopped, plus more whole leaves for garnish
2	tablespoons fresh cilantro leaves
¼	cup (60 ml) extra-virgin olive oil, plus more for drizzling
	Salt and freshly ground black pepper

In a blender, combine half of the coarsely chopped tomatoes, cucumber, and onion with the avocado, jalapeño, garlic, lime juice, and 1 cup (240 ml) cold water and blend until smooth. Transfer the puree to a large bowl.

Add the remaining coarsely chopped tomatoes, cucumber, and onion to the blender along with the mint, cilantro, and oil and pulse to a chunky puree. Add the puree to the bowl and stir well. Refrigerate the soup until well chilled, about 1 hour.

Season the soup with salt and pepper to taste. Garnish with tomato wedges, diced cucumber, and mint leaves, and finish with a drizzle of oil. Serve cold.

chilled beet soup with yogurt and pepitas SERVES 4

In 2006, I took the trip of a lifetime to South Africa. I fell in love with the country and its food. One day we went to a popular restaurant in Cape Town called Lucy's, and I had a beet soup so delicious that as soon as I got home I had to try to re-create the flavors. It is the perfect first course, or serve it in shot glasses as an hors d'oeuvre—it's on the rich side, so you don't need a lot per serving. If you want to make this soup in a hurry, look for vacuum-sealed roasted red beets in the produce section. They're so much better than canned beets.

1   pound (455 g) roasted or boiled red beets, coarsely chopped

1   cup (240 ml) light coconut milk

2   teaspoons fresh lime juice

1   teaspoon finely grated peeled ginger

1   teaspoon salt

    Freshly ground black pepper

4   teaspoons plain nonfat Greek yogurt

4   teaspoons roasted, salted pepitas (hulled pumpkin seeds) or sunflower seeds

Put the beets, coconut milk, lime juice, ginger, salt, and pepper to taste in a blender and puree until very smooth. Transfer to a container and chill until ready to serve.

To serve, pour about ¾ cup (180 ml) soup into each of four small glasses; top each serving with 1 teaspoon yogurt and 1 teaspoon pepitas and serve immediately.

grilled chicken paillard with arugula and shaved pecorino SERVES 4

This recipe is one of the simplest but most satisfying in this book, especially for anyone trying to watch their "summer figure." I am a big fan of pounding chicken breasts out thin, not only because they cook more evenly and are more tender, but also because it makes me feel like I'm getting a bigger portion. I know, it's all in my head, but nonetheless it works. This makes a perfect lunch, or you can serve it to company at dinner on a platter with the salad piled high on top.

4   boneless, skinless chicken breast halves

Extra-virgin olive oil

Salt and freshly ground black pepper

¼   teaspoon garlic powder

Grated zest and juice of ½ lemon

½   teaspoon grainy mustard

8   cups (160 g) arugula or mixed greens

Shaved Pecorino Romano cheese

Preheat an outdoor grill to high. (If you hold your hand about 3 inches [7.5 cm] from the grill grate, you should have to move it within 3 seconds.)

Arrange a chicken breast between two sheets of plastic wrap. Using a meat mallet or small heavy pan, pound the chicken evenly until it is ¼ inch (6 mm) thick. Remove the plastic wrap and repeat with the remaining chicken breasts; put the paillards on a baking sheet and brush both sides of each piece lightly with oil. In a small bowl, combine 1 teaspoon salt, ½ teaspoon pepper, and the garlic powder and sprinkle it evenly over both sides of the chicken pieces.

Lightly oil the grill grate with an oil-soaked towel. Grill the chicken, turning once, until cooked through and grill marks appear, about 2 minutes per side. Transfer to a clean platter.

In a large bowl, whisk the lemon zest and juice, the mustard, and 2 tablespoons oil until combined; season with salt and pepper to taste. Add the arugula to the bowl and toss to evenly coat.

Put a piece of chicken on each of four plates and top with a mound of arugula. Garnish with cheese and more pepper to taste and serve immediately.

salmon salad with lemon dijon caper vinaigrette SERVES 4

I eat salmon a couple times a week and am always looking for different ways to prepare it (though often I get in a rut and just season it with salt, pepper, and chili powder, bake it, and call it a day). This salad, based on tender Bibb lettuce, is nice and delicate, and the vinaigrette is quite light, making it ideal for lunch.

For the salad:

8	ounces (225 g) salmon fillet
	Salt and freshly ground black pepper
1	head Bibb lettuce, torn into pieces
2	ribs celery, thinly sliced
1	cup (55 g) thinly sliced English cucumber
¼	cup (25 g) roughly chopped fresh flat-leaf parsley
2	tablespoons minced fresh chives

For the vinaigrette:

1	tablespoon fresh lemon juice
1	tablespoon Dijon mustard
3	tablespoons extra-virgin olive oil
	Zest of 1 lemon
1	tablespoon capers, roughly chopped
	Splash of white wine vinegar
	Salt and freshly ground black pepper

Make the salad: Preheat the oven to 350°F (175°C). Spray a baking dish with nonstick cooking spray.

Season the salmon with salt and pepper. Place on the baking dish and bake for 15 to 20 minutes, until the fish flakes easily with a fork. Let cool. Remove and discard the skin and flake the flesh with a fork.

In a salad bowl, combine the lettuce, celery, cucumber, parsley, chives, and salmon.

Make the vinaigrette: In a small bowl, whisk the lemon juice and mustard until emulsified. Add the oil and whisk. Stir in the lemon zest, capers, and vinegar and season with salt and pepper to taste.

Add the vinaigrette to the salad and toss well. Serve immediately.

soba noodle salad SERVES 4-6

Don't get me wrong, I love a pasta salad made with mayo and some random chopped veggies, but sometimes I like to mix it up a bit and prepare something different, like this soba noodle salad. It is an excellent side dish to serve with grilled fish or chicken and also doubles as a main course for vegetarians.

12	ounces (340 g) dried soba noodles or spaghetti
½	cup (130 g) creamy peanut butter
¼	cup (60 ml) soy sauce
¼	cup (60 ml) rice vinegar or white wine vinegar
2	tablespoons fresh lime juice
2	teaspoons toasted sesame oil
2	cloves garlic, finely minced
1	teaspoon finely grated peeled ginger
1	cup (about 3 ounces/85 g) snow peas, thinly sliced lengthwise
1	cup (110 g) grated or julienned carrots (about 2)
1	red bell pepper, cored and thinly sliced lengthwise
4	scallions, white and green parts, thinly sliced
1	tablespoon toasted sesame seeds (optional)

Cook the noodles according to the package instructions, drain, and rinse.

While the noodles are cooking, in a small saucepan over low heat, whisk the peanut butter, soy sauce, vinegar, lime juice, sesame oil, garlic, and ginger together until the peanut butter melts and the dressing is smooth.

In a large bowl, combine the noodles and dressing, tossing until evenly coated. Add the peas, carrots, red pepper, scallions, and sesame seeds, if using, and toss gently until evenly distributed. Serve at room temperature or chill in the refrigerator and serve cold.

spinach salad with pickled strawberries and poppyseed dressing SERVES 4-6

Strawberries in a spinach salad: good. Pickled strawberries in a spinach salad: better. Pickled strawberries and poppyseed dressing in a spinach salad: best.

For the dressing:

- ²/₃ cup (165 ml) canola oil
- ¹/₃ cup (75 ml) apple cider vinegar
- 3 tablespoons honey
- 2 tablespoons Dijon mustard
- 1 large egg
- ½ teaspoon salt
- ¼ teaspoon freshly ground black pepper
- 2 tablespoons poppy seeds

For the salad:

- 1 cup (165 g) sliced strawberries
- ½ cup (120 ml) red wine vinegar
- 1 bay leaf
- 1 tablespoon sugar
- 1 teaspoon salt
- ¼ teaspoon freshly ground black pepper
- 10 ounces (280 g) spinach
- ½ red onion, thinly sliced
- 1 cup (95 g) thinly sliced white button mushrooms

Make the dressing: Put the oil, vinegar, honey, mustard, egg, salt, and pepper in a blender and blend until smooth. Stir in the poppy seeds. Refrigerate until ready to serve.

Make the salad: Put the strawberries in a nonreactive heatproof bowl. In a small saucepan over medium heat, combine the vinegar, ½ cup (120 ml) water, the bay leaf, sugar, salt, and pepper. Bring to a low boil and allow the sugar to dissolve. Pour over the strawberries and let stand for about 20 minutes. Remove the bay leaf and drain the strawberries, discarding the liquid.

In a large salad bowl, combine the spinach, onion, mushrooms, and strawberries. Pour the dressing over the salad, toss well, and serve immediately.

kale caesar salad SERVES 4

I really love Caesar salads, especially when kale is involved (All hail kale!), but making the dressing can be a bit of a pain. My pal Geoffrey Zakarian made a Caesar dressing on *The Kitchen* that was similar to this one; I loved the way it tasted and that it was so easy to put together. Anchovy paste is one of those ingredients that some people wrinkle their nose at (I used to be one of those people, until my ex-husband used it in an awesome marinade for steak and got me hooked), but it adds a real depth of flavor. I keep a tube of it in my fridge and use it here and there to amplify the flavors in my cooking.

½   cup (120 ml) mayonnaise

4   tablespoons (30 g) grated Parmesan cheese

1   tablespoon fresh lemon juice

1   tablespoon red wine vinegar

1   tablespoon anchovy paste

1   tablespoon drained capers

¼   teaspoon freshly ground black pepper

1   bunch Tuscan kale, stemmed, leaves sliced into ribbons

Croutons (recipe follows)

In a blender or food processor, combine the mayonnaise, 2 tablespoons of the cheese, the lemon juice, vinegar, anchovy paste, capers, and pepper and blend until smooth.

In a large salad bowl, toss the kale and croutons with the dressing. Top with the remaining 2 tablespoons cheese and serve.

i am kale obsessed!

croutons

MAKES 2 CUPS (80 G)

2   tablespoons unsalted butter, melted

2   tablespoons olive oil

½   teaspoon garlic salt

½   teaspoon dried oregano

2   cups (1-inch/2.5-cm) cubed crusty Italian bread

Preheat the oven to 350°F (175°C).

In a large bowl, whisk the butter, oil, garlic salt, and oregano together. Add the bread cubes and toss to coat. Spread in a single layer on a baking sheet. Bake for 10 to 15 minutes, until golden brown and toasted. Remove from the oven and let cool completely.

kale pesto

MAKES 1 1/2 CUPS (250 G)

Because I just can't get enough kale, I had to make it into a pesto. This kale pesto is bright green and tastes as vibrant as it looks. I added some flax seeds for an extra oomph of nutrients, but if you don't have any, just use some extra walnuts.

¼   cup (25 g) walnut halves

2   tablespoons flax seeds

3   cloves garlic

3   cups (50 g) packed chopped kale

1   tablespoon fresh lemon juice

½   teaspoon sea salt

½   teaspoon freshly ground black pepper

¾   cup (180 ml) extra-virgin olive oil

½   cup (60 g) grated Pecorino Romano cheese

In a food processor, pulse the walnuts, flax seeds, and garlic together. Add the kale and pulse to puree. Add the lemon juice, salt, and pepper and pulse to combine. With the motor running, slowly add the oil and process until smooth. Pulse in the cheese. The pesto can be refrigerated in an airtight container for up to one week.

great on pasta, grilled chicken, or with eggs

vietnamese beef and noodle salad bowls SERVES 4

I really like serving this to a group: I put all of the items in separate bowls and let people make their own combinations. It's always fun when guests can customize. If you have a lazy Susan, put all the toppings on it, set it in the middle of the table, and let the fun begin.

3	tablespoons plus ¼ cup (60 ml) fish sauce
2	tablespoons brown sugar
1	tablespoon grated garlic
1	tablespoon grated peeled ginger
1	pound (455 g) flank steak, thinly sliced against the grain
½	cup (120 ml) fresh lime juice
¼	cup (60 ml) honey
1	small red chile, thinly sliced
1	tablespoon canola oil
1	(8.8-ounce/250-g) package rice vermicelli noodles, cooked according to package instructions
1	English cucumber, diced
2	carrots, grated
1	head green leaf lettuce, thinly sliced
1	bunch fresh cilantro (leaves only)
1	bunch fresh mint (leaves only)

In a medium bowl, whisk the 3 tablespoons fish sauce, the brown sugar, garlic, and ginger together. Add the steak and toss to coat. Let marinate for 30 minutes at room temperature, or up to 4 hours in the refrigerator.

In another bowl, whisk the remaining ¼ cup (60 ml) fish sauce, the lime juice, honey, and chile together. Set aside until ready to serve (this will be your dressing).

Remove the beef from the marinade and pat dry with a paper towel. Reserve the marinade. Heat the oil in a wok or large skillet over high heat. Quickly stir-fry the beef for about 2 minutes. Add the reserved marinade and toss to coat, making a quick glaze. Remove from the heat.

Serve the beef, noodles, dressing, cucumber, carrots, lettuce, cilantro, and mint in individual bowls and let everyone make their own salad.

salade niçoise SERVES 4

I always say that food is like music; it's nostalgic. Just like when you hear a song and it takes you back to a certain moment in your life, eating something can transport you as well. This salade niçoise takes me right to the South of France on a warm summer day. I always use canned tuna for salade niçoise, not seared tuna, which has become so common on menus. If you prefer seared, though, by all means, go for it!

For the dressing:

- 1 tablespoon Dijon mustard
- 1 tablespoon red wine vinegar
- 3 tablespoons extra-virgin olive oil

  Salt and freshly ground black pepper

- 1 teaspoon minced fresh flat-leaf parsley

For the salad:

  Salt

- 12 ounces (340 g) new potatoes or very small red potatoes
- 8 ounces (225 g) French green beans, trimmed and cut into thirds

  Freshly ground black pepper

- ½ head green leaf lettuce, chopped (about 6 cups)
- 1 cup (150 g) grape tomatoes, halved
- ½ cup (90 g) pitted Kalamata olives, halved
- 4 hard-cooked eggs, peeled and quartered
- 12 ounces (340 g) good-quality tuna packed in oil, drained and flaked into large chunks

  Oil-packed anchovies (optional)

Make the dressing: In a small bowl, whisk the mustard and vinegar together until combined. Add the oil and whisk until emulsified; season with salt and pepper to taste and whisk in the parsley.

Make the salad: Bring a saucepan filled with water to a boil and salt it generously. Add the potatoes and cook until tender when pierced with a knife, 12 to 15 minutes. Using a slotted spoon, transfer the potatoes to a large bowl to cool briefly. Drop the green beans into the water and cook until crisp-tender, about 1 minute; drain. When the potatoes are just cool enough to handle but still warm, cut them into bite-size pieces and put them in a large bowl.

Add the green beans to the warm potatoes, drizzle a little dressing over them, season with salt and pepper, and toss to combine. Add the lettuce, tomatoes, and olives; pour the remaining dressing over the vegetables and toss to coat.

Transfer the lettuce mixture to a serving platter and season with salt and pepper. Arrange the eggs and tuna evenly over the salad and garnish with anchovies, if using. Serve immediately.

chinese chicken salad SERVES 4-6

The dressing for this salad makes me think of a restaurant that I worked at in college, Kona Bistro, in Oxford, Ohio. We served what we called a Thai chicken salad, but the dressing was made with hoisin sauce, which is Chinese, so go figure. I make this version (inspired by Wolfgang Puck's Chinois Chicken Salad) on hot summer days, and its crunchy vegetables are so satisfying and hydrating in the heat.

For the salad:

Breast meat of 1 store-bought rotisserie chicken

½ small head Napa cabbage, thinly sliced crosswise

½ small head iceberg lettuce, shredded

1 red bell pepper, cored and thinly sliced lengthwise

2 cups (about 4 ounces/115 g) bean sprouts

1 (8-ounce/227-g) can sliced water chestnuts, coarsely chopped

6 scallions, white and green parts, thinly sliced

½ cup (30 g) coarsely chopped fresh cilantro leaves

1 cup (55 g) crispy chow mein noodles

½ cup (75 g) roasted unsalted soybeans or peanuts

2 large navel oranges

Salt and freshly ground black pepper

For the dressing:

2 tablespoons fresh orange juice

2 tablespoons hoisin sauce

2 tablespoons rice vinegar

1 small clove garlic, grated

1 teaspoon grated peeled ginger

3 tablespoons vegetable oil

Salt and freshly ground black pepper

Make the salad: Remove the skin from the chicken and shred the meat with a fork. In a large bowl, toss the chicken, cabbage, lettuce, red pepper, bean sprouts, water chestnuts, scallions, cilantro, chow mein noodles, and peanuts together. With a sharp knife, cut the peel from the orange, cut the segments away from the membrane, coarsely chop them, and add them to the bowl. Slice the other orange in half and squeeze over a small bowl, reserving 2 tablespoons of juice.

Make the dressing: In a small bowl, whisk the reserved orange juice, hoisin sauce, vinegar, garlic, and ginger together. While whisking, slowly add the oil and whisk until emulsified and thick; season with salt and pepper to taste.

Pour the dressing over the salad, season with salt and pepper. Toss and serve.

thai cod cakes

I got on an Asian cooking kick for a few weeks and I was testing out all sorts of recipes. I invited a few friends over to try out my new cuisine, including Bobby Flay. Now, it was maybe not the best idea to try new recipes out on Bobby Flay, an Iron Chef. What was I thinking? I was more than a little nervous, but I calmed myself down and went on, with confidence. And guess what? He loved everything I made, especially these Thai-inspired cod cakes. The red curry paste adds just the right touch of heat without overpowering the fresh fish, and the sweet chili sauce is a nice balance to the spice.

1	pound (455 g) fresh wild cod fillet
4	scallions, white and green parts, finely chopped
¼	cup (10 g) fresh cilantro leaves, finely chopped
	Salt and freshly ground black pepper
1	large egg
1 ¼	teaspoons Thai red curry paste
1	teaspoon fish sauce
1	cup (115 g) panko bread crumbs
	Vegetable oil for frying
	Sweet Thai chili sauce

you can substitute other firm white fish for the cod!

Chop the cod into large chunks and put it in a food processor. Pulse until the fish breaks down into little chunks, but do not pulverize it; transfer the fish to a large bowl. Add the scallions and cilantro, season lightly with salt and pepper, and stir to combine.

In a small bowl, whisk the egg, curry paste, and fish sauce together until very smooth. Add the egg mixture to the fish and stir gently until completely combined. Pour the panko into a shallow dish and season it lightly with salt. Divide the fish mixture into eight equal portions and form them into disks about 1 inch (2.5 cm) thick. Dredge the fish cakes in the panko, pressing it on all sides to adhere and placing them on a plate as you dredge them. Chill the cakes in the refrigerator for at least 30 minutes, or up to overnight.

Pour about ¼ inch (6 mm) of oil into a medium nonstick skillet and heat it over medium heat. Working in batches, gently slip the fish cakes into the oil and fry, turning once, until golden brown and cooked through, 2 to 3 minutes per side. Drain on paper towels and season lightly with salt. Serve immediately, with chili sauce on the side.

grilled escarole salad with citrus

SERVES 4

When it comes to grilling, greens usually aren't a big part of most people's repertoires. But I'm telling you, they're great for grilling. Try a grilled romaine Caesar salad, for example, or this grilled escarole with citrus. The escarole holds up really well on the grill, and the smoky flavor is a nice complement to the oranges. This salad is hearty enough to be served on its own for lunch, or add a piece of grilled salmon for dinner.

4   small heads escarole, halved lengthwise

Extra-virgin olive oil

Salt and freshly ground black pepper

Fresh lemon juice

1   fennel bulb, cored and thinly sliced on a mandoline, plus 1 tablespoon fronds, coarsely chopped

1   small red onion, thinly sliced on a mandoline

1   navel orange, peeled, pith removed, cut into segments

1   ruby grapefruit, peeled, pith removed, cut into segments

Preheat an outdoor grill to medium.

Brush the escarole with oil and season with salt and pepper. Place the escarole cut side down on the grill and cook until it begins to char and the leaves have wilted, about 3 minutes. Remove from the heat, season with a squeeze of lemon juice, and arrange two halves on each of four plates.

In a bowl, toss the fennel, fennel fronds, onion, and orange and grapefruit segments together until combined. Drizzle with 1 tablespoon oil and a squeeze of lemon juice; season with salt and pepper and toss to combine.

Arrange the fennel-fruit mixture over the top of the escarole on each plate and serve immediately.

WINTER SQUASH FACTOID:

did you know winter squash is
harvested in late summer
but gets its name because
it lasts through winter?

late summer farro, butternut squash, and arugula salad SERVES 4-6

Feeling stressed? Eat this salad. No, seriously: Farro has a high magnesium content, which can help relieve tension. It's also really high in fiber. Butternut squash is often found pre-cut in supermarket produce sections, and it starts popping up at farm stands toward the end of the summer. This recipe is also delicious in the fall using pumpkin or other autumn squash varieties.

1 **pound (455 g) butternut squash, peeled and cut into ½-inch (12-mm) chunks (about 4 cups)**

2 **large shallots, sliced**

4 **tablespoons (60 ml) extra-virgin olive oil**

Salt and freshly ground black pepper

½ **cup (85 g) golden raisins**

2 **tablespoons sherry vinegar**

1 **teaspoon grainy mustard**

Pinch of ground cayenne

1 **cup (190 g) farro, cooked according to the package instructions and cooled**

3 **ounces (85 g) smoked Gouda cheese, very finely diced**

½ **cup (50 g) walnut halves, toasted and coarsely chopped**

3 **cups (60 g) arugula**

Preheat the oven to 375°F (190°C). Line a baking sheet with parchment paper.

Put the squash and shallots on the prepared baking sheet and drizzle 1 tablespoon of the oil over them. Toss well with your hands to coat. Season with salt and pepper and roast, tossing halfway through, until the squash is soft and the shallots are beginning to brown, 25 to 30 minutes. Let cool to room temperature.

Meanwhile, put the raisins in a shallow bowl and pour the vinegar over them. Soak, tossing them every now and then, for at least 15 minutes. Drain the vinegar into another small bowl, squeezing the raisins to remove any excess.

Whisk the mustard into the vinegar. While whisking, add the remaining 3 tablespoons oil in a slow stream until thick and emulsified. Season the dressing with the cayenne and salt and pepper to taste.

To assemble the salad, in a medium bowl, toss the farro, squash and shallots, raisins, cheese, and walnuts together until combined. Pour the dressing over the salad, season with salt and pepper, and toss until evenly coated with dressing. Just before serving, fold in the arugula.

lentil salad SERVES 4

In St. Bart's, the Hotel Taïwana is the place to be come lunchtime. It's steps from the ocean, and everyone comes up from the beach for a break from the sun and the best lunch on the island. My order is the same every time. I always get the barbecue chicken and the lentil salad. Oh, the lentil salad! It is so simple, yet so perfect (and at 22 euros a pop, it should be perfect). They serve it with toasted baguette, spread with tangy Dijon mustard and sliced white onions. I like to pile a big spoonful of lentils onto the baguette for a just-right bite. Here's my take on it.

1 ½	cups (290 g) dried lentils
3	large shallots, halved lengthwise, plus 1 tablespoon minced shallot
1	large clove garlic, smashed
1	small bay leaf
3	tablespoons red wine vinegar
1 ½	teaspoons Dijon mustard, plus more for serving
3	tablespoons extra-virgin olive oil
	Salt and freshly ground black pepper
8	long slices baguette, toasted
	Shaved sweet white onion
	Hot pepper vinegar

Put the lentils in a saucepan with the halved shallots, the garlic, and bay leaf and enough water to cover them by at least 3 inches (7.5 cm). Bring to a boil over medium-high heat. Reduce the heat to a low simmer, cover, and cook until the lentils are soft but still hold their shape, about 20 minutes.

Drain the lentils in a fine-mesh sieve and discard the shallots, garlic, and bay leaf. Transfer the lentils to a bowl and cover to keep warm.

In a small bowl, whisk the vinegar, mustard, and minced shallots together until combined. Add the oil and whisk until thick and emulsified; season with salt and pepper to taste. Pour the dressing over the warm lentils and gently stir until the dressing is absorbed. Taste and adjust the seasoning with salt and pepper if needed.

To serve, spread a thin layer of mustard on each of the toasted baguette slices and scatter some of the onion over each. Divide the lentils among four salad plates, with two dressed baguette toasts on each plate, and offer pepper vinegar for sprinkling over the top at the table.

grilled zucchini, corn, black bean, and avocado salad SERVES 4

A plate of grilled vegetables can be a kind of boring side dish, but if you chop 'em up and turn them into a salad, they sing. With the black beans, this salad is not only an excellent side dish, it's also a great main dish to serve if you have vegetarian friends joining. I also like this salad with a sprinkling of grated ricotta salata or crumbled feta cheese.

1	medium zucchini (about 10 ounces/280 g), sliced lengthwise into slabs ½ inch (12 mm) thick
	Extra-virgin olive oil
	Salt and freshly ground black pepper
1	large ear of sweet corn, husked
1	bunch scallions
1	(15-ounce/425-g) can black beans, drained and rinsed
1	ripe avocado, diced
	Juice of ½ lemon
	Juice of ½ lime
1	teaspoon Dijon mustard
1	teaspoon honey
½	teaspoon dried oregano

Preheat an outdoor grill to medium-high.

Brush the zucchini slices lightly with oil and season lightly with salt and pepper. Grill the slices, turning once, until charred but not mushy, about 2 minutes per side. Grill the corn, turning frequently, until cooked through and the kernels are charred, about 10 minutes. Grill the scallions whole, turning them frequently, until charred and soft, about 2 minutes.

Cut the zucchini into ½-inch (12-mm) pieces and put them in a serving bowl. Slice the kernels from the corn and add them to the zucchini; chop the scallions and add them also. Add the beans and avocado to the bowl and toss gently to combine.

In a small bowl, whisk the lemon and lime juices, the mustard, honey, and oregano together. While whisking constantly, add about 2 tablespoons oil in a slow stream; whisk until thick and emulsified. Season the dressing with salt and pepper to taste and pour it over the vegetables. Toss well to coat, taste, and season with more salt and pepper if necessary. Serve immediately.

lobster reubens

I never had a lobster roll until I moved to the Hamptons. In fact, I had never even had lobster until I came here. Now I love lobster rolls. A lobster roll is pretty simple: lobster meat, mayo, bun. My friend Keith came home from a trip to Florida and was raving about a lobster reuben he had eaten. My mind got going and I couldn't stop thinking about it. You can use store-bought sauerkraut if you want to go the totally traditional reuben route here, but it can be a bit strong next to the mild, sweet lobster meat, so I favor making a simple vinegar slaw instead. You decide!

For the slaw:

- 1 **cup (70 g) very thinly shredded Savoy or white cabbage**
- 1 **tablespoon rice vinegar**
- ½ **teaspoon sugar**

  Salt and freshly ground black pepper to taste
- ⅛ **teaspoon celery seeds**

For the sandwiches:

- ¼ **cup (60 ml) mayonnaise**
- 2 **teaspoons ketchup**
- 2 **teaspoons sweet pickle relish, well drained**
- ¼ **teaspoon paprika**
- 1 **pound (455 g) cooked lobster meat, coarsely chopped**
- 8 **slices rye or marbled rye sandwich bread**
- 8 **thick slices Swiss cheese**
- 3 **tablespoons unsalted butter, at room temperature**

Make the slaw: Put the cabbage in a small bowl. Sprinkle the vinegar, sugar, salt, pepper, and celery seeds over the top and toss well. Let stand, tossing frequently, until the cabbage wilts, about 20 minutes.

Make the sandwiches: In a small bowl, stir together the mayonnaise, ketchup, relish, and paprika. Add half of the dressing to the lobster meat and toss well to combine. Arrange the bread slices on a work surface and spread a little of the remaining dressing on each slice. Put a slice of cheese on each piece of bread; divide the lobster meat among four of the slices. Top each sandwich with one quarter of the slaw and invert the remaining cheese-covered bread slices onto each sandwich. Spread ½ tablespoon softened butter on the top of each sandwich.

Melt the remaining 1 tablespoon butter in a large nonstick skillet over medium heat and swirl the pan to coat it. Arrange the sandwiches, butter side up, in the pan and cook until the bottom is golden, about 5 minutes. Carefully flip the sandwiches and cook until the underside is golden brown and the cheese is melted, about 5 minutes more.

Remove the sandwiches from the pan and let stand for a minute before slicing on the diagonal and serving warm.

burgers,

tacos

+

pizza

Burgers, tacos, and pizza, OH MY! Seriously.

I was trying to figure out where to include these three foods—they're certainly not light meals, they can be dinner, but they can also be lunch. They really deserve their own chapter, right?

I could eat all three for the rest of my life and never get tired of them. You know when people ask, "If you were stranded on a desert island and could only have one food." I would take burgers, tacos, or pizza. But what if you had a hybrid of all three? A pizza topped with a burger that was folded like a taco? Well, that sounded better in my head, but, alas, this is not a stoner cookbook.

All three hold a special place in my heart/stomach. Let's start with the burger. In 2008, at the first Burger Bash of the New York City Wine & Food Festival, in a complete surprise victory, I won. I made my Logan County Burger (it's basically a grilled cheese with a thin burger tucked inside). I never imagined the controversy that my silly little burger could cause. A prominent chef (who will remain nameless) asked for a recount, *New York Magazine* did a story questioning if it was truly a burger since it's on toasted white bread and not a bun, and Frank Bruni of the *New York Times* made a video with me demonstrating the Logan County Burger. I think people liked it because it was simple; there wasn't a lot of stuff on it and it was easy to eat.

Let's talk tacos: I have had a love affair with them nearly my whole life. When I was a teenager and the cool thing to do was to walk aimlessly around the mall for hours, I would ask my mom for lunch money. She'd hand me two bucks and tell me to eat at Taco Bell. I'd get sixty-nine cent tacos and a (free) ice water and I was happy as a clam. Later I learned that Taco Bell isn't exactly authentic (no offense, Dorito Loco taco), and I spent some quality time in Mexico surfing and sampling tacos.

As for pizza, now that's amore. I LOVE pizza. GOOD pizza. The summer after my sophomore year of college, I took off for a semester in Florence. Our school partnered with a local restaurant, and we got vouchers for a two-course meal every night. Now, the smart thing to do would have been to order something like a salad and a pasta or pizza, or an antipasto and a grilled fish or chicken. Nope. Every Tuesday, Wednesday, and Thursday nights (those were the days we had class—on weekends we took off to backpack and stay in questionable hostels), I had pasta AND pizza. Then I would walk next door for a gelato. Let's just say, my mom commented on my plumpness when I stepped off the plane.

These days I make pizza often using my outdoor pizza oven or on my grill. And I've learned a little self-control . . .

blt ranch burgers MAKES 4 BURGERS

Did I say BLT *and* ranch *and* burger? All three in one recipe? Yep. I made these burgers for a group of friends one afternoon and they pretty much lost their minds. The ranch dressing is rich and creamy next to the beefy burger with that crispy bacon, lettuce, and tomato. They are truly indulgent!

For the dressing:

1	cup (240 ml) mayonnaise
½	cup (120 ml) plain yogurt
¼	cup (60 ml) buttermilk
2	tablespoons minced fresh chives
2	tablespoons minced fresh flat-leaf parsley
¼	teaspoon salt
¼	teaspoon freshly ground black pepper
¼	teaspoon garlic powder

For the burgers:

1	pound (455 g) lean ground beef
1	tablespoon Worcestershire sauce
1	large egg, lightly beaten
½	teaspoon salt
¼	teaspoon freshly ground black pepper
4	potato buns, buttered and toasted
8	pieces cooked bacon, cut in half
1	ripe tomato, sliced
	Bibb lettuce leaves

Make the dressing: Combine all the dressing ingredients and mix well. Refrigerate until ready to serve.

Make the burgers: Preheat an outdoor grill to medium-high.

In a bowl, combine the beef, Worcestershire sauce, egg, salt, and pepper. Shape into four patties.

Grill the patties for about 3 minutes per side for medium doneness.

Place each patty on a bun and top with bacon, tomato, lettuce, and a generous dollop of dressing. Close the burgers with the top bun half and serve immediately.

Bring extra napkins, y'all

shrimp
burger

turkey
burger

shrimp burgers with old bay mayo MAKES 4 BURGERS

Shrimp and *burger* are two words that don't usually go side by side, but trust me: You will be so happy if you make these. The texture is similar to a crab cake, but on the firmer side. They are so good, if I do say so myself. And the Old Bay mayo? Ohhhhh myyyyyy.

For the mayo:

- ½ cup (120 ml) mayonnaise
- 2 teaspoons Old Bay seasoning

For the burgers:

- 1 pound (455 g) medium shrimp, peeled and deveined
- 1 large egg, lightly beaten
- ⅔ cup (80 g) panko bread crumbs
- 2 scallions, white and green parts, thinly sliced
- 1 tablespoon fresh lemon juice
- ½ teaspoon salt
- ¼ teaspoon freshly ground black pepper
- ¼ teaspoon garlic powder
- ¼ cup (60 ml) canola oil
- 4 brioche buns, lightly toasted
- 1 tomato, sliced
- Lettuce leaves
- 1 avocado, sliced

Make the mayo: In a small bowl, whisk the mayonnaise and Old Bay. Refrigerate until ready to serve.

Make the burgers: Coarsely chop half of the shrimp. Put the remaining shrimp in a food processor and pulse until smooth. In a large bowl, combine the chopped and pureed shrimp with the egg, bread crumbs, scallions, lemon juice, salt, pepper, and garlic powder; mix well. Refrigerate for 10 minutes, then shape into four patties. Place on a plate and refrigerate for 10 minutes longer.

Heat the oil in a large skillet over medium-high heat. Add the patties and cook for 3 to 4 minutes per side, until the shrimp is opaque throughout. Spread the buns with the mayo and add the burgers, topped with tomato, lettuce, and avocado. Serve immediately.

turkey burgers with caramelized onions, cheddar, and peach chipotle ketchup

MAKES 4 BURGERS

My friend Bennett told me about a burger he used to eat in college so often that the diner renamed it the Benny Burger. It was a beef patty with grilled onions, melted cheddar and ketchup. These days, he's not a red meat eater, so I felt inspired to give the original a makeover. I didn't used to be much on turkey burgers, but this grown-up Benny Burger changed my mind.

For the ketchup:

- 1 cup (185 g) diced ripe peaches
- 1 cup (240 ml) ketchup
- 1 chipotle chile in adobo
- 1/2 teaspoon ground cinnamon

For the burgers:

- 1 pound (455 g) ground dark meat turkey
- 1 large egg, lightly beaten
- 2 tablespoons grated onion
- 1 tablespoon Dijon mustard
- 1 tablespoon Worcestershire sauce
- 1/2 teaspoon salt
- 1/4 teaspoon freshly ground black pepper
- 1/4 teaspoon garlic powder
- 1 tablespoon olive oil
- 2 onions, halved and thinly sliced
- 8 slices cheddar cheese
- 4 onion buns, buttered and toasted

  Lettuce leaves

Make the ketchup: Put all the ketchup ingredients in a blender and blend until smooth. Refrigerate until ready to serve.

Make the burgers: In a bowl, combine the turkey, egg, grated onion, mustard, Worcestershire sauce, salt, pepper, and garlic powder. Shape into four patties. Cover and refrigerate for 20 minutes.

In a large skillet, heat the oil over medium-high heat. Add the sliced onions and sauté until they begin to wilt, about 4 minutes. Reduce the heat to low and continue cooking until caramelized, 10 to 15 minutes. If the onions start to burn at any point, add a tablespoon of water at a time.

Preheat an outdoor grill to medium-high. Cook the burgers for about 5 minutes. Flip and cook on the other side for about 2 minutes, until cooked through. Top each with some of the caramelized onions and two slices of cheese. Cover the grill and cook for about 2 minutes longer, until the cheese is melted. Place on the buns and serve with the ketchup and lettuce.

italian sausage and pepper burgers MAKES 4 BURGERS

When I was a kid, my dad used to make sausage burgers all the time on the grill. He used breakfast sausage, so I thought why not do Italian sausage with the onions-and-peppers bit? The pickled banana peppers are the star addition to this burger—the acid cuts right through the fat of the sausage and gives it a nice little zing.

1 tablespoon olive oil

1 onion, thinly sliced

1 red bell pepper, cored and thinly sliced

1 clove garlic, minced

1 tablespoon tomato paste

8 ounces (225 g) hot Italian sausage (if links, remove casings)

8 ounces (225 g) sweet Italian sausage (if links, remove casings)

8 slices provolone cheese

4 ciabatta rolls, lightly toasted

¼ cup (60 ml) pesto

Pickled banana peppers

Heat the oil in a large skillet over medium heat. Add the onion, pepper, and garlic and sauté until the onion is translucent and the pepper is tender, 8 to 10 minutes. Stir in the tomato paste and cook for 1 minute longer. Remove from the heat.

Preheat an outdoor grill to medium-high. Combine both sausages in a bowl. Form into four patties. Grill for 4 to 5 minutes per side, until cooked through. Top each burger with some of the onions and peppers and two slices of cheese, cover the grill, and cook until the cheese melts. Spread the rolls with pesto, add the burgers and banana peppers, and serve immediately.

tacos!

steak tacos with pickled radishes and mashed avocados SERVES 4-6

A couple of summers ago, I did a pop-up taco truck for a week. I made a taco similar to this one, and it was a hit. I love the flavor combo of the pickled peppery radishes with the steak and the creaminess of the avocados.

For the pickled radishes:

2	bunches radishes, tops removed, thinly sliced
1	white onion, thinly sliced
1¼	cups (300 ml) distilled white vinegar
2	tablespoons sugar
1	teaspoon kosher salt

For the steak:

½	cup (120 ml) fresh lime juice
½	cup (120 ml) olive oil
2	tablespoons chili powder
1	tablespoon garlic paste
2	pounds (910 g) skirt steak
	Salt and freshly ground black pepper

For the avocados:

2	avocados
½	teaspoon salt
	Juice of 1 lime

For serving:

White corn tortillas, warmed (see note)

Fresh cilantro

Make the pickled radishes: Put the radishes and onion in a nonreactive heatproof bowl or container. In a saucepan, bring the vinegar, 1¼ cups (300 ml) water, the sugar, and salt to a boil. Pour over the radishes and onion. Let cool completely. Refrigerate until ready to serve.

Make the steak: In a large bowl, whisk the lime juice, oil, chili powder, and garlic paste together. Add the steak and toss to coat. Cover and refrigerate for at least 1 hour, or up to overnight.

Preheat an outdoor grill to medium-high. Meanwhile, mash the avocados: Cut the avocados in half, pit them, and scrape the flesh into a bowl. Mash well, then stir in the salt and lime juice.

Remove the steak from the marinade and season with salt and pepper. Put the steak on the grill and cook, flipping once, for about 8 total minutes for medium doneness. Remove to a carving board, let stand for a few minutes, then thinly slice on the diagonal.

To build each taco, spoon some of the mashed avocado onto a tortilla and top with steak, radishes and onions, and cilantro. Serve immediately.

Note: To warm the tortillas, brush a hot griddle with oil and heat the tortillas on each side to brown them up a bit. Wrap them in foil to keep them hot until it's time to eat.

adobo chicken tacos with pico de gallo and grilled corn SERVES 4-6

These tacos are a universal crowd pleaser—everyone loves a chicken taco. Pico de gallo is so simple to put together and the taste is far superior to any salsa you could buy in a jar. Cotija cheese is available at most grocery stores these days, but if you can't find it, try feta or farmers' cheese as a substitute.

For the chicken and corn:

- ½ cup (120 ml) olive oil
- ½ cup (120 ml) fresh lime juice
- 1 chipotle chile in adobo, minced
- 2 tablespoons adobo sauce (from the can of chipotles)
- 1 tablespoon garlic paste
- 2 pounds (910 g) boneless, skinless chicken thighs
- Salt and freshly ground black pepper
- 2 ears corn, husked

For the pico de gallo:

- 2 large ripe tomatoes, finely diced
- 1 white onion, finely diced
- ½ jalapeño, minced
- ½ bunch fresh cilantro (leaves only), minced
- Juice of ½ lime
- Salt and freshly ground black pepper

For serving:

- White corn tortillas, warmed (see note, page 84)
- Iceberg lettuce, shredded
- Cotija cheese
- Sour cream

Make the chicken and corn: In a large bowl, whisk the oil, lime juice, chipotle, adobo sauce, and garlic paste together. Add the chicken and toss to coat. Cover and refrigerate for at least 1 hour, or up to overnight.

Preheat an outdoor grill to medium-high. Remove the chicken from the marinade and season with salt and pepper. Put the chicken on the grill and cook, flipping once, until cooked through, about 5 to 6 minutes per side. Remove to a carving board and slice on the diagonal. Grill the corn until just marked on all sides and cut the kernels from the cobs into a bowl.

Make the pico de gallo: In a medium bowl, combine the tomatoes, onion, jalapeño, cilantro, and lime juice and season with salt and pepper to taste.

To build each taco, place some chicken on a tortilla and top with lettuce, pico de gallo, corn, cheese, and a drizzle of sour cream. Serve immediately.

grilled smoky tofu tacos with black beans, peach cucumber salsa, and lime sour cream SERVES 4-6

Meat eaters, do not be skeptics of the smoky tofu taco. I'm telling you, the flavors are bonkers. In fact, I cooked several different kinds of tacos for a group of friends (none vegetarian), and these actually were the favorite. The peach cucumber salsa is super yummy and refreshing. You can also try it as an accompaniment to grilled fish or chicken.

For the lime sour cream:

- 1 cup (240 ml) sour cream
- Juice of ½ lime

For the salsa:

- 3 yellow peaches, finely diced
- 1 small cucumber, peeled, seeds removed, finely diced
- ½ red onion, finely diced
- ½ jalapeño, minced
- ½ bunch fresh cilantro, minced
- Juice of ½ lime
- Salt and freshly ground black pepper

For the black beans:

- 1 yellow onion, minced
- 1 tablespoon olive oil
- 4 cloves garlic, minced
- 2 teaspoons chili powder
- 1 teaspoon ground cumin
- Pinch of red pepper flakes
- 1 tablespoon tomato paste
- 2 (14-ounce/392-g) cans black beans, drained and rinsed
- Salt and freshly ground black pepper

For the tofu:

- 2 (8-ounce/227-g) packages smoked tofu
- Olive oil

For serving:

- White corn tortillas, warmed (see note, page 84)

Make the lime sour cream: In a small bowl, whisk the sour cream and lime juice together and transfer to a squeeze bottle, if you like, or a container. Refrigerate until ready to serve.

Make the salsa: In a large bowl, combine the peaches, cucumber, onion, jalapeño, cilantro, and lime juice and season with salt and pepper to taste. Set aside.

Make the black beans: In a large skillet, sauté the onion in the oil until translucent, about 5 to 7 minutes. Add the garlic, chili powder, cumin, and red pepper flakes. Cook for 2 minutes, then stir in the tomato paste. Add the beans and ½ cup (120 ml) water. Bring to a simmer, reduce the heat to low, and cook for 10 minutes. Season with salt and pepper. Use a potato masher or the back of a wooden spoon to partially mash the beans. Cover to keep warm, or reheat when ready to serve.

Make the tofu: Preheat an outdoor grill or grill pan to medium-high.

Brush the tofu on both sides with oil. Grill for 2 to 3 minutes per side, to heat through, then transfer to a carving board and slice.

To build each taco, spoon some beans onto a tortilla. Top with tofu and salsa. Drizzle with lime sour cream and serve immediately.

fish tacos with creamy chipotle sauce and pico de gallo SERVES 4-6

When I was writing the novel *Groundswell*, I spent a month in Mexico to "research." Translation: I spent a month in Mexico eating fish tacos and surfing. I tried almost every taco stand in town, except one, because I thought it looked too touristy. It was always packed, so finally I decided to give it a shot. Wow wow wow: It was off-the-charts good. They served their tacos with a variety of sauces in squeeze bottles, and my personal favorite was a chipotle sauce. It was creamy, slightly spicy, tangy, with a hint of sweetness. As soon as I got back home, I set off to re-create it. This is pretty darn close. Fish tacos are typically made with fried fish, but I like cooking the fish in a skillet to keep it lighter, although you could certainly fry yours if you wish.

For the chipotle sauce:

- 1 cup (240 ml) mayonnaise
- 2 chipotle chiles in adobo

  Juice of 1 lime
- 1 tablespoon honey
- 2 tablespoons chopped fresh cilantro

  Pinch of salt

For the fish:

- 1 1/2 pounds (680 g) flaky white fish, such as mahi-mahi or cod, cut into 4-ounce (115-g) fillets
- 4 tablespoons (60 ml) olive oil

  Juice of 1 lime
- 1 tablespoon chili powder
- 1 teaspoon garlic salt

For serving:

  White corn tortillas, warmed (see note, page 84)

  Purple cabbage, shredded

  Fresh cilantro
- 1 recipe pico de gallo (see page 85)

Make the chipotle sauce: Combine all the ingredients in a food processor and blend until creamy and smooth. Transfer to a squeeze bottle, if you like, or a container and refrigerate until ready to serve.

Make the fish: In a bowl, combine 2 tablespoons of the oil, the lime juice, chili powder, and garlic salt. Toss with the fish and marinate for 15 minutes.

In a large skillet, heat the remaining 2 tablespoons oil over medium-high heat. Add the fish and cook for 3 to 4 minutes per side. Remove to a plate and flake with a fork.

To build each taco, spoon some fish onto a tortilla. Top with sauce, cabbage, cilantro, and pico de gallo.

una pizza napoletana

MAKES 1 (10-INCH/25-CM) PIZZA, PLUS SAUCE FOR MORE

Last year I decided to go to pizza school. I enrolled in a class taught at the Los Angeles chapter of the Associazione Verace Pizza Napoletana. (I know, pizza in LA? I asked why the class was held there rather than in New York, and apparently the Italians preferred the weather in LA.)

I went into the class thinking I knew about pizza. I have a pizza oven in my backyard and I make pizzas all summer long. After about an hour in pizza school, I realized I had been doing it all wrong. I had been making pizza more difficult than it needed to be. I would always cook a sauce, but here I learned I could just use high-quality canned tomatoes with a little sea salt. I also made a more complicated dough with more ingredients than necessary, and stretching it out was always a challenge. I would usually roll it with a rolling pin, which I learned is a big no-no. A rolling pin will push all of those nice air bubbles right out of the dough and change the texture for the worse.

I was amazed at the precision of true Neapolitan pizza making. The ingredients were weighed, the sauce applied using the back of a spoon in a clockwise motion, the cheese scattered moving from the center out to the edges, two hand-torn basil leaves tossed atop the cheese, and extra-virgin olive oil drizzled from a carafe in the shape of a backward six. My obsession with pizza grew, and I find it to be one of the most relaxing meals to make. I love working with dough; it feels so good in my hands and makes me feel calm. Plus, at the end, you get to eat pizza, something I could do every single day and never get tired of it.

The most important thing to remember when you're making pizza is to work with confidence. Like many things in life, hesitation can trip you up. Don't be intimidated of the dough; work like you mean it.

1   (28-ounce/794-g) can whole peeled tomatoes, preferably San Marzano, drained

    Sea salt

    Double-zero ("00") flour or all-purpose flour for shaping the dough

1   (9-ounce/255-g) ball of Pizza Dough (recipe follows), at room temperature

2   ounces (55 g) fresh mozzarella cheese, torn into strips

2   large fresh basil leaves

Set a pizza stone on the lowest rack of the oven, remove the other racks, and preheat to 500°F (260°C).

Using a food mill, grind the tomatoes into a bowl (or pulse in a food processor until coarsely pureed). Season with salt and set aside.

Very lightly dust a work surface with some flour. Fill a medium bowl with flour and spread it out into a wide even layer. Drop the dough onto the flour in the bowl and flip it over once in the bowl to lightly coat it. On the work surface, using your fingertips, press the dough all over to flatten it. Flip it over and press all over the surface again. Flip it one more time and repeat. Press the dough with your fingers repeatedly on one side with one hand, and with the other hand, slowly turn the dough clockwise on the work surface. Continue poking and rotating the dough to flatten and stretch the dough.

Pick the dough up and toss it back and forth between the palms of your hands until it begins to stretch, forms a rough disk, and gets thinner. Drape the dough over your hands, tuck your fingers in, and gently pull your knuckles toward the outer edge of the dough. Continue, rotating the dough as you go, until it is about 10 inches (25 cm) in diameter. Work slowly, allowing the weight of the dough itself to stretch the circle. Do not force it or the dough will tear and the crust can become too chewy.

Dust the work surface with a little more flour and set the dough back down. Press it with your fingers and pull it gently at the edges to even out the circle. Using a small ladle, evenly spread about ¼ cup (60 ml) of the tomato sauce over the surface of the dough, leaving a ½-inch (12-mm) border around the edges. Scatter the mozzarella pieces from the center out, leaving space between the cheese. (My teacher told me to think of the cheese as "little islands" on the pizza.) Tear the basil leaves in half and scatter the pieces over the pizza.

Lightly flour a pizza peel (or a thin rimless baking sheet) and set it on the work surface at the edge of the pizza crust closest to you. (You may want to have a friend hold it on the edge of the counter for you.) Run your fingers around the outside parameter of the crust to loosen any edges that might be stuck (and make sure the dough is not stuck to the counter anywhere in the center). Gently grab the dough at the 5 o'clock and 7 o'clock positions and in one quick motion, pull the pizza onto the peel. (Do this with confidence!) Use your fingers to pull and straighten the crust until round.

Open the oven door. Set the front of the peel on the back edge of the pizza stone. Shake the peel very lightly to make sure the dough is not stuck and will slide. Holding the peel at a 45-degree angle, jiggle it until the pizza begins to slide off; once it reaches the edge of the peel, shake the peel lightly a few times and then pull it out in one swift motion to drop the pizza onto the hot stone. Immediately close the oven door and cook until the crust begins to char on the bottom and edges and the cheese is melted and bubbly, 8 to 10 minutes.

Use the peel to remove the pizza; slide it onto a cutting board. Slice with a pizza wheel and serve immediately.

pizza dough

MAKES 4 (9-OUNCE/255-G) BALLS OF
DOUGH, ENOUGH FOR 4 PIZZAS

- .10   ounce (3 g) fresh cake yeast
- 2 ½   cups (600 ml) bottled spring water, at room temperature
- .9   ounce (25 g) sea salt
- 2   pounds (910 g) double-zero ("OO") flour), plus more as needed (about 7 cups)

Put the yeast in a measuring cup and dissolve it in about ½ cup (120 ml) of the water. In a large bowl, dissolve the salt in the remaining water.

Add about ½ cup (65 g) of the flour to the salt-water solution and add the yeast mixture. Use your fingers to mix well. Add the remaining flour and mix with your hands until it forms a dough. Transfer the dough to a floured countertop.

To knead the dough, grab the sides with your fingers and pull it up and over itself into the center. Using the balls of your hands, press the dough firmly in the center. Repeat, pulling the dough from the outer sides inward. Press it fast from the edge inward. Working quickly will help prevent it from sticking. Continue kneading the dough until it is very smooth to the touch and springs back when pressed, 15 to 20 minutes. Shape the dough into a ball, place it in a clean bowl, and cover with plastic wrap.

Let the dough rise for 2 hours, then divide it into four 9-ounce (255-g) portions. Shape the portions into balls. Cover the dough with a towel and let rise at room temperature for 6 hours.

grilled pizza MAKES 1 (10-INCH/25-CM) PIZZA

Grilled pizza? Yes. I first had grilled pizza at a restaurant in Providence, Rhode Island, called Al Forno. Everything on the menu there is outstanding, but the grilled pizza is otherworldly. The first time I went there, I must have eaten about six pizzas on my own. The dough gets crispy on the outside from the hot grill, but stays chewy on the inside. It's insanely good. Don't be intimidated by working with dough on the grill. The key to success is a clean grill; the dough won't stick to clean grill grates. And as always, when working with pizza dough, work with confidence!

9 ounces (255 g) Pizza Dough (page 93), formed into a 10-inch (25-cm) circle according to the instructions on page 92

Your choice of pizza toppings

Cheese

Extra-virgin olive oil

Preheat an outdoor grill to medium-high.

Place the pizza dough on the grill. Cook for about 1 minute, then flip with tongs (the dough will "release" itself when it's ready to flip). Move the crust to a cooler spot on the grill (about medium heat). Top with desired toppings and the cheese. Cover the grill and cook until the cheese is melted and the crust is crisp, 3 to 4 minutes. Use tongs to remove the pizza to a carving board and drizzle with oil. Cut into slices and serve.

when i'm in a hurry, i use store-bought dough... shhh...

94   burgers, tacos, and pizza

Cocktail hour

A proper cocktail hour feels very civilized, doesn't it? Whether I'm straight from the beach, still salty and smelling like suntan lotion, or I'm dressed and it's the start of a dinner party, making drinks and having a nibble with friends just feels good. The first clink of glasses is like the clock chiming "Let the good times begin."

One of my favorite cocktail hour snacks is microwaved popcorn. I'm not talking about the kind that comes in a box and leaves your fingers coated with yellow dust. I take a paper bag from the grocery store, fill it with ½ cup kernels, a splash of olive oil or a spoonful of liquid coconut oil, and a sprinkle of salt. I fold the top of the bag down, leaving plenty of air and space for the corn to pop. Into the microwave for 3 to 4 minutes, and out comes perfectly popped corn. I drizzle the popcorn in the bag with melted butter, add more salt and a seasoning (I like Parmesan cheese, Chinese five-spice powder, chili powder, or even lime zest), give it a shake, and pour it into a serving bowl. It's always a crowd pleaser.

frozen blueberry daiquiris SERVES 4

A cocktail packed with antioxidants? This blueberry daiquiri certainly fits that bill, and I'm all for it!

½	cup (100 g) sugar
1	pint (335 g) blueberries
2	cups (480 ml) rum
¼	cup (60 ml) fresh lime juice
2	cups (480 ml) ice

In a medium saucepan over medium-high heat, combine the sugar and ½ cup (120 ml) water and bring to a low boil, stirring until the sugar dissolves. Add the blueberries and reduce the heat to a simmer. Use a wooden spoon to crush the berries, allowing their juices to release, and continue to simmer for 20 minutes. Press the berry mixture through a fine-mesh sieve set over a bowl and discard the solids.

In a blender, combine the berry syrup, rum, and lime juice. Add the ice and blend until smooth. Serve immediately.

watermelon-rum punch MAKES ABOUT 2 QUARTS; SERVES 8

Rum punch is one of those drinks that sneaks up on you. When I serve it, I turn on some Bob Marley and we sit out on the back porch and just chill. Rum makes you feel all warm and happy—especially when it's combined with watermelon! The bubbly ginger beer lightens it all up and gives a little spicy kick. If you have a crowd, this recipe is easily doubled or tripled. And here's a shortcut: If you don't feel like breaking down a whole watermelon, most produce sections sell watermelon that's already been cut into cubes.

1 ½	pounds (680 g) cubed seedless watermelon (about 8 cups), plus more wedges for garnish
1	cup (240 ml) fresh orange juice
¼	cup (60 ml) fresh lime juice
1	cup (240 ml) light rum
1	(12-ounce/360-ml) bottle ginger beer
	Thin orange slices

Put the cubed watermelon in a blender and blend until liquefied. Pour the mixture through a very-fine-mesh sieve into a large pitcher and discard the solids. Add the orange juice, lime juice, and rum and stir well. Chill until ready to serve.

To serve, add the ginger beer and float orange slices in the punch. Fill rocks glasses with ice, pour in the punch, and garnish each glass with a watermelon wedge.

aperol spritz

SERVES 6-8

Aperol is an Italian orange liqueur usually served, as the name implies, as an apéritif. I had my first Aperol spritz after a Vespa ride through Greenwich Village with Mario Batali. He took me to his restaurant Otto and served me the drink along with some sliced prosciutto. It was a warm day, and the drink was cool and refreshing. It quickly became my summer cocktail of choice. Mario garnished his with a green olive, and that's how I like mine, though I've never seen it done that way anywhere else so I always ask the bartender for it. I usually get a look like "Huh?" and I say, "Trust me, it's really good."

When I make these in a pitcher for a group, I use three parts prosecco, two parts Aperol, and a splash of club soda, as below; if I'm making them individually, I just eyeball it.

3 cups (720 ml) prosecco

2 cups (480 ml) Aperol

Club soda

Orange slices or green olives

In a pitcher, combine the prosecco and Aperol. Top with club soda. Serve chilled or over ice and garnish each drink with an orange slice or green olive.

prosciutto-wrapped figs and gorgonzola

MAKES 16; SERVES 8

Salty-sweet, my favorite combo. These are incredibly simple to make, but my friends go nuts for them. I like serving these at cocktail time, usually with an Aperol spritz. I'm not a fan of cheese plates before dinner because they tend to be too filling, but I do love cheese, so these are a nice compromise. I get to have my cake (well, cheese) and eat it, too. If you can't find fresh figs, try using sliced peaches.

2 ounces (55 g) Gorgonzola cheese (I like to use Gorgonzola dolce, the creamy kind)

8 figs, halved

8 slices prosciutto, cut in half lengthwise

Pinch off a small piece of Gorgonzola and place it on top of a fig half. Wrap a piece of prosciutto around it. Repeat with the remaining fig halves and serve.

deviled egg spread SERVES 6

It's not a party at my house without deviled eggs. They're simple to make, but sometimes I just don't feel like going to the trouble of making the filling, putting it in a piping bag, filling the eggs, then making sure they don't get messed up when I cover them and store them in the fridge before serving. The solution to my deviled egg-making woes? A spread!

1	dozen large eggs
2	tablespoons distilled white vinegar
8	ounces (225 g) sliced white sandwich bread
1	cup (240 ml) mayonnaise
1	tablespoon yellow mustard
	Salt and freshly ground pepper
	Paprika

Preheat the oven to 450°F (230°C).

In a large saucepan, cover the eggs with water, add the vinegar, and bring to a rapid boil. Cover the saucepan and remove it from the heat; let stand for 15 minutes. Drain the eggs and cool them under cold running water, shaking the pan vigorously to crack the shells. Let the eggs cool in the water.

Meanwhile, quarter the bread slices on the diagonal and arrange them in a single layer on a large baking sheet. Toast the bread in the oven for about 6 minutes, turning once, until barely browned. Let cool.

Peel the eggs and halve them lengthwise. Coarsely chop half of the egg whites and transfer them to a large bowl. Add the remaining egg whites and all of the yolks to a food processor along with the mayonnaise and mustard and process until smooth. Scrape the mixture into the bowl and blend with the chopped egg whites. Season with salt and pepper to taste.

Top the toast points with the egg spread and dust lightly with paprika. Arrange the toasts on a platter and serve. Alternatively, serve the egg spread in a bowl with the toast points alongside.

crispy chickpeas

SERVES 4-6

These chickpeas are the ideal snack at cocktail hour—crispy, salty, and smoky. The recipe is easily changed up, too: If you don't want to do the smoked paprika, try cumin, chili powder, or Chinese five-spice powder, or just keep it simple with some sea salt. The possibilities are endless—just be sure to always, always have them with an ice-cold something or other.

1   (15-ounce/425-g) can chickpeas, drained and rinsed

½   cup (120 ml) olive oil

     Smoked paprika

     Garlic salt

Pat the chickpeas dry with paper towels (this will ensure crispy results). Heat the oil in a medium skillet over medium-high heat. Add half of the chickpeas and fry, stirring occasionally, until golden brown, 2 to 3 minutes. Use a slotted spoon to remove them to a paper towel–lined plate. Repeat with the remaining chickpeas. While still warm, season with a sprinkle each of paprika and garlic salt. Serve warm or at room temperature.

black bean and peach salsa scoops

SERVES 6-8

Black beans and peaches are an unlikely combo, I know, but I promise they are a match made in heaven. My mom used to make quesadillas with black beans, peaches, and cheese; I think she got the idea from a magazine, and we thought it sounded so strange we had to try it. They were a hit, and so are these little bite-size scoops.

1   cup (170 g) canned black beans, drained and rinsed

1   cup (185 g) diced peaches

2   tablespoons minced red onion

1   tablespoon minced fresh cilantro

1   clove garlic, minced

     Salt and freshly ground black pepper

     Tortilla scoop chips

Combine the beans, peaches, onion, cilantro, and garlic in a medium bowl. Season with salt and pepper to taste. Spoon the mixture into tortilla scoops and serve immediately.

fresh
pineapple-
coconut
martinis →

cucumber
with chile flakes,
flaky sea salt
+ lemon ↓

cherry
lillet
blanc
spritz

←

pimento
goat
cheese
spread

↙

pimento goat cheese spread SERVES 4-6

Ask a Southerner about pimento cheese and the usual response will go something like this: "Ooohhh"—eyes roll back in head—"I looooove pimento cheese." Typically, it's made with just cheddar cheese, pimentos, mayo, and maybe a little pickle relish, sometimes a touch of cream cheese (or, in my grandpa's recipe, a little Velveeta). Now, I'm a firm believer in the old adage "If it ain't broke, don't fix it," but I got to thinking about adding some goat cheese to the traditional recipe and came up with this gem. It's really easy, great for dipping crudités for cocktail hour, or spread between two pieces of bread for a sandwich, or smeared on the bun for your burger.

- 1   (11-ounce/310-g) log fresh goat cheese, softened
- 4   ounces (115 g) smoked cheddar cheese, shredded (1 packed cup)
- ½   cup (120 ml) mayonnaise
- ¼   cup (50 g) drained jarred pimentos, coarsely chopped
- 2   scallions, white and green parts, thinly sliced
- 1   tablespoon sweet pickle relish
- 1   teaspoon onion powder
- 1   teaspoon Tabasco sauce
     Salt and freshly ground black pepper
     Halved radishes and celery sticks

In a medium bowl, using a wooden spoon, blend the goat cheese with the cheddar cheese, mayonnaise, pimentos, scallions, pickle relish, onion powder, and Tabasco sauce; season with salt and pepper. Transfer to a bowl and serve with radishes and celery.

cherry lillet blanc spritz SERVES 2

Lillet is a liqueur from the Bordeaux region that I typically only drink in the summer. It's fruity and refreshing, and the French typically drink it over ice with a slice of orange, lemon, or lime. I find that it works really well in cocktails, especially when club soda is involved—the bubbles lighten it up a bit. It pairs nicely with the Bing cherries in this cocktail, but you can try substituting other berries if you so desire.

- 8   fresh Bing cherries, pitted and halved, plus 2 cherries on the stem for garnish
- 3   orange slices
     Pinch of sugar
- ½   cup (120 ml) Lillet Blanc
- ½   cup (120 ml) club soda, or to taste

Fill two rocks glasses with ice.

Put the pitted cherries, 1 of the orange slices, and the sugar in a cocktail shaker and muddle until the cherries are broken down and juicy. Add the Lillet, fill the shaker half full with ice, and shake until very cold.

Divide the mixture between the glasses, top with club soda, garnish each drink with a whole cherry and an orange slice, and serve.

fresh pineapple-coconut martinis

SERVES 4, WITH PINEAPPLE-INFUSED
VODKA LEFT OVER

By now we've all heard how good coconut water is for us: It's hydrating, it has potassium, and so on. Well, did you know that pineapple makes you feel calm? Yep, it's high in serotonin, which helps you feel calm and can aid in sleep (much like melatonin). So, I figure, why not combine the two and add vodka for good measure? Plan ahead for this recipe, as you'll be infusing vodka with pineapple, which takes at least three days. You can use the pineapple vodka for these martinis or you can just serve it on ice with a splash of club soda.

For the pineapple vodka:

- 1   fresh pineapple, peeled, cored, and cut into rings
- 1   (750-ml) bottle of your favorite vodka

For the martinis:

- 1   cup (240 ml) unsweetened pure coconut water
- 2   teaspoons light agave syrup or simple syrup
- 1   cup (240 ml) homemade pineapple vodka

  Pineapple wedges

Make the pineapple vodka: Put the pineapple slices in a tall, narrow pitcher with a lid or beverage dispenser and pour the vodka over it. Be sure the pineapple is completely submerged. Cover tightly and set aside at room temperature for at least 3 days and up to 1 week.

Make the martinis: In a pitcher, stir the coconut water and agave together until dissolved. Add the vodka and stir. Pour half of the mixture into an ice-filled cocktail shaker and shake vigorously until very cold. Strain into two chilled martini glasses, garnish with pineapple wedges, and serve. Repeat with the remaining martini mixture and fresh ice.

cucumber with chile flakes, flaky sea salt, and lemon SERVES 4

It's a challenge to come up with a dish that's spicy, salty, and refreshing all at once, but these cucumbers do just that. Pair with a cocktail on a sultry evening and you've got yourself a winner!

- 1   English cucumber, cut into ¼-inch (6-mm) rounds

    Red chile flakes

    Flaky sea salt (I like Maldon)

- ½   lemon

Put the cucumber slices on a platter and sprinkle with chile flakes, sea salt, and a squeeze of lemon juice.

corn fritters SERVES 4-6

Tell me: What is better than fresh corn in the summer? I cook it every which way I can, and these corn fritters are a star recipe. I serve them at cocktail hour with a simple dollop of sour cream and scallions, but the sky is the limit. You could top them with caviar, with tomatoes and basil, or serve them for breakfast with maple syrup, or even as dessert with fruit and whipped cream.

3	large eggs, separated, yolks lightly beaten and whites beaten to stiff peaks
1 ½	cups (250 g) corn kernels, cut from the cob
¼	cup (35 g) cornmeal
¼	cup (30 g) all-purpose flour
½	teaspoon salt
½	teaspoon baking powder
	Canola oil for frying
	Sour cream
2	Scallions, white and green parts, thinly sliced

Mix the egg yolks with the corn, cornmeal, flour, salt, and baking powder. Fold in the beaten egg whites.

Heat a few tablespoons of the oil in a large skillet over medium-high heat. Using a small ice cream scoop, drop mounds of the batter into the hot oil. Fry until golden brown and cooked through, about 2 minutes, then flip and fry for 2 minutes more. Transfer the fritters to a paper towel–lined plate. Fry the remaining batter in batches, adding more oil to the skillet as needed. Serve hot, garnished with sour cream and scallions.

painkillers SERVES 2

A couple of years ago, I went down to Tortola for a quick surf trip with a few friends. We took a boat over to Jost Van Dyke for a day trip to the Soggy Dollar Bar. We pulled up, jumped overboard, and swam up to the beachside bar (hence "soggy dollar"). As I lay in a hammock after lunch, sipping on a painkiller cocktail, all my cares seemed a million miles away.

- ½ cup (120 ml) dark rum, such as Pusser's
- 1 cup (240 ml) pineapple juice
- ¼ cup (60 ml) fresh orange juice
- ¼ cup (60 ml) canned cream of coconut

   Freshly grated nutmeg

   Pineapple and orange slices

Fill two hurricane glasses with ice.

In a cocktail shaker, combine the rum, pineapple juice, orange juice, and coconut cream and shake.

Divide the mixture between the glasses and grate nutmeg over each. Garnish each with a slice of pineapple, a slice of orange, and a paper umbrella.

mojito slushies SERVES 4

Who doesn't love a slushie on a hot summer evening? Slushies make me feel like a kid, except that these are definitely for grown-ups. Please note that this recipe takes some advance planning, as a few hours are needed to freeze the mojito mixture.

- ¼ cup (10 g) fresh mint leaves
- 1 (12-ounce/355-ml) can limeade concentrate, thawed
- 1 cup (240 ml) light rum

   Lime slices

Put the mint in a freezer-safe pitcher and, using the end of a wooden spoon or cocktail muddler, mash the leaves well to release their oils and roughly chop them up. Add the limeade, 1 quart (960 ml) water, and the rum and freeze.

After 2 hours, stir the mixture to combine. Freeze for an additional 2 hours and stir again. Remove the slushie from the freezer 15 to 20 minutes before serving. If there are any large ice chunks, pulse them in a food processor until slushy and drinkable.

Divide among chilled glasses, garnish with lime slices, and serve.

coconut shrimp SERVES 4-6

Dave's Grill in Montauk is my favorite restaurant on Long Island. I go there when I want to feel like I'm on vacation and totally relax. Everything on the menu is incredible, and most of it stays the same year to year, but there are always some additions and some dishes that disappear. They used to have coconut shrimp as an appetizer and served it with marmalade, and I miss it so much that I have to make my own now! Be sure not to overcook the shrimp or it will get rubbery.

24	large shrimp (about 1 pound/ 455 g; 21- to 25-count), peeled and deveined, tails left on
	Salt and freshly ground black pepper
½	cup (60 g) cornstarch
3	large egg whites, beaten until slightly foamy
2	cups (180 g) unsweetened coconut flakes
	Canola oil for frying
½	cup (120 ml) orange marmalade

Put the shrimp in a bowl, season with salt and pepper, and toss well. Sprinkle the cornstarch over the shrimp, toss them in the bowl to coat them evenly, shake the excess off each shrimp, and transfer them to a plate.

Put the egg whites in a shallow dish and the coconut in another shallow dish. Dip the starch-coated shrimp in the egg whites to coat, and then in the coconut, pressing it to adhere.

Fill a deep, heavy saucepan with 3 inches (7.5 cm) of oil and heat the oil to 350°F (175°C). Working in batches and adjusting the heat to maintain the temperature, fry the shrimp, turning them occasionally, until golden brown and cooked through, 2 to 3 minutes. Drain on a paper towel–lined plate. Lightly season the shrimp with salt while still warm.

Stir the marmalade and 1 tablespoon water together in a glass bowl and heat on high power in the microwave for 30 seconds (or heat in a small saucepan until the marmalade liquefies). Serve the shrimp warm with the marmalade on the side for dipping.

radishes with butter

Sometimes the simplest things in life are the best. Am I right? Let some butter come to room temperature so it's nice and creamy, then slice some radishes in half, spread with the butter, and sprinkle with flaky sea salt. Ahhhh . . . the spicy flavor of the radish is mellowed by the rich butter and the salt brings it all together. Serve with an ice-cold apéritif.

honeydew margaritas

SERVES 2

I love trying different kinds of margaritas when I go to restaurants, but often they're too sweet or have too much tequila. I've taken to making margaritas at home; it's really fun to experiment with seasonal fruits, like honeydew in the summer. This is a really nice, light margarita. Just be sure to use good-quality tequila!

1/4	whole honeydew, seeded, peeled, and cut into chunks (about 2 cups/340 g)
3	tablespoons fresh lime juice
1	tablespoon orange liqueur, such as Cointreau
1/2	cup (120 ml) silver tequila
1	teaspoon light agave syrup
1	teaspoon sugar
1/2	teaspoon coarse salt
	Lime wedges

Put the honeydew in a blender and blend until smooth. Pour into a large cocktail shaker. Add the lime juice, orange liqueur, tequila, and agave syrup.

On a small plate, combine the sugar and salt. Rub the rims of two rocks glasses with a lime wedge and dip the rims into the sugar mixture to adhere. Add a handful of ice cubes to the shaker and shake until very cold. Fill the sugar-rimmed glasses with ice, strain the cold margaritas into them, and serve.

dinner

I love a theme party. I'm pretty sure it goes back to my days as social chair in my sorority, when I used to plan parties with themes like "Bikers and Babes" or "Heaven and Hell." (Luckily for my guests, my tastes have graduated.) When it's dinner-party time, I choose a theme, such as Italian or Moroccan, and base my menu and table around it—I even choose music to go along. I find that it makes planning easier for me because it narrows down my choices.

One of my most memorable parties was a Jamaican night. It was late summer and I cranked up the reggae, grilled Jerk chicken, and had plenty of Red Stripe to go around. We had so much fun . . . so much fun that the neighbors thought we were too loud and the police showed up. Maybe not as much has changed since those sorority parties as I thought . . .

fisherman's platter SERVES 4-6

Oh boy, do I love a fried fisherman's platter. When I was a little kid, my grandparents would take us on a once-a-year trip to Myrtle Beach. We looked forward to that trip all year long. My grandpa liked to go to the Sea Captain's House for a special dinner; it was right on the beach. He loved fried seafood, especially oysters. This recipe makes me think of him.

Vegetable oil for frying

2 pounds (910 g) mixed fresh seafood (firm fish fillets such as cod or hake, large shrimp, shucked oysters, clam strips, or whole shucked clams)

¾ cup (105 g) fine cornmeal

½ cup (55 g) all-purpose flour

1 teaspoon baking powder

1 teaspoon salt

1 teaspoon paprika

¼ teaspoon garlic powder

¼ teaspoon freshly ground black pepper

1 cup (240 ml) milk

Tartar sauce

Cocktail sauce

Lemon wedges

Fill a Dutch oven or heavy deep saucepan with at least 3 inches (7.5 cm) of oil and heat the oil to 375°F (190°F) over medium-high heat.

Cut the fish into large chunks about 2 inches (5 cm) long.

In a shallow dish, combine the cornmeal, flour, baking powder, salt, paprika, garlic powder, and pepper. Pour the milk into another shallow dish. Dip the seafood in the milk, then dredge it in the cornmeal mixture, shaking off the excess. If you like a thicker breading, repeat the process, dipping the seafood in the milk and cornmeal mixture again.

Working in batches, lower the seafood into the hot oil and fry, turning frequently, until golden brown, about 3 minutes for fish fillets, and 1 ½ to 2 minutes for shrimp, oysters, and clams. Transfer the hot seafood to a paper towel–lined plate to drain. Serve immediately with tartar sauce, cocktail sauce, and lemon wedges.

cuban turkey in the caja china...

Roasting Box

MODEL #3

™

LA CAJA CHINA

®

www.lacajachina.com

insanely good

cuban turkey in the caja china with sweet and sour pineapple marmalade SERVES 10

OK, if you haven't heard of the Caja China, get familiar. Do not pass go, do not collect $200, go directly to Google. These things are like magic boxes; they could not be easier to use and food typically cooks faster. A turkey, a pork butt, chickens, a whole pig—whatever goes in comes out with insanely crispy skin and unbelievably moist, fall-apart meat. I cannot explain how this happens, but it is as if a magician has waved a magic wand.

For this turkey, I make a marinade very similar to what Cubans would use to inject a whole pig before roasting. If you don't have an injector, I highly recommend purchasing one (they are inexpensive and easy to find). You can use it to inject roasts as well, and it will make a big difference. And if you don't have a Caja China (yet), just roast the turkey in the oven (but seriously consider a Caja China!).

1   (14-pound/6.3-kg) turkey, giblets and neck removed

For the rub:

2   tablespoons kosher salt

2   teaspoons dried oregano

2   teaspoons freshly ground black pepper

For the marinade:

1   cup (240 ml) pineapple juice

½   cup (120 ml) fresh orange juice

½   cup (120 ml) fresh lime juice

¼   cup (60 ml) olive oil

2   tablespoons Worcestershire sauce

1   tablespoon kosher salt

2   teaspoons garlic powder

2   teaspoons onion powder

2   teaspoons dried oregano

2   teaspoons freshly ground black pepper

2   teaspoons ground cumin

For the marmalade:

½   cup (120 ml) fresh orange juice

¼   cup (60 ml) white wine vinegar

3   tablespoons brown sugar

2   cups (330 g) chopped pineapple

2   tablespoons minced red onion

1   jalapeño, minced

Salt and freshly ground black pepper

For serving:

12-14 buns (optional)

Pat the turkey dry with paper towels. Combine the rub ingredients in a small bowl and rub the turkey with the mixture on the inside and outside.

Make the marinade: Put all the marinade ingredients in a blender and blend to combine. Fill an injector with the mixture and inject the turkey all over. It will plump with the fluid.

Place the turkey, breast side down, in a disposable aluminum pan. Put the pan inside the Caja China box. Place the lid tray in position and build a charcoal fire in the tray (I use a chimney starter to make this easy). Roast the turkey in the box (no peeking!) for 1 ½ hours, continuously adding charcoal as it burns out. You will use about 8 pounds (3.6 kg) of charcoal per hour.

While the turkey is roasting, make the marmalade: In a medium saucepan over medium-high heat, whisk the orange juice, vinegar, 2 tablespoons water, and the brown sugar until the sugar dissolves. Add the pineapple, onion, and jalapeño. Bring to a low boil, then reduce the heat to a simmer. Simmer, stirring occasionally, until the mixture has thickened, about 15 to 30 minutes. Season to taste with salt and pepper.

Carefully remove the lid from the Caja China (have a safe place to set it down, as the charcoal is still burning on top). Use tongs to flip the turkey breast side up. Replace the lid and allow the turkey to roast for another 40 minutes, until the internal temperature of the thigh meat reaches at least 165°F (75°C). Remove the turkey and tent it with foil for 15 minutes. Slice and serve on buns if desired, with pan juices and pineapple marmalade.

tuna with romesco sauce SERVES 4-6

This is a dish that is ideal for entertaining, as it is equally delicious served hot or cold, and it takes almost no time at all to prepare. The tuna needs only a few minutes to cook, and the romesco actually benefits from being made ahead of time to allow the flavors time to develop.

For the romesco sauce:

2	jarred roasted red peppers
½	cup (75 g) almonds
1	slice bread
2	tablespoons red wine vinegar
1	tablespoon honey
1	teaspoon smoked paprika
½	cup (120 ml) extra-virgin olive oil
	Salt and freshly ground black pepper

For the tuna:

1 ½	pounds (680 g) very fresh tuna steaks
1	tablespoon olive oil
	Salt and freshly ground black pepper

Make the romesco sauce: In a food processor, combine the red peppers, almonds, bread, vinegar, honey, and smoked paprika. Pulse to combine. With the motor running, add the oil. Season with salt and pepper to taste.

Make the tuna: Preheat an outdoor grill or a grill pan to medium-high. Drizzle the tuna with oil and generously season with salt and pepper on both sides. Sear for about 2 minutes on each side. Remove from the grill, tent with foil, and let stand for a few minutes. Thinly slice the tuna and serve with the romesco sauce.

grilled chicken parmesan SERVES 4

OK, so, confession time. In the winter, I eat chicken Parmesan weekly, sometimes more often. Next to pizza, it's probably my favorite food. It can be kind of fattening, though. I mean, it is breaded, fried, and covered in melted cheese. It's not exactly warm-weather food, but I crave those flavors in the summer too. So I started making it on the grill. It's much lighter this way, the perfect summer fare: grilled chicken, a little tomato sauce, and fresh mozzarella.

4   boneless, skinless chicken breast halves

Extra-virgin olive oil

1   teaspoon salt

½   teaspoon freshly ground black pepper

¼   teaspoon garlic powder

1   cup (240 ml) marinara sauce (I use Rao's if I don't have time to make homemade)

Fresh mozzarella cheese

Preheat an outdoor grill to medium-high. Make sure the grates are clean so the chicken doesn't stick.

Arrange a chicken breast between two sheets of plastic wrap. On a work surface, using a meat mallet or small heavy pan, pound the chicken evenly until it is ¼ inch (6 mm) thick. Remove the plastic wrap and repeat with the remaining chicken breasts; put them on a baking sheet. Brush both sides of each lightly with oil. In a small bowl, combine the salt, pepper, and garlic powder and sprinkle it evenly over both sides of the chicken breasts.

Place the chicken on the grill and cover the grill. Cook for 3 to 4 minutes. Flip and spread a few tablespoons of marinara sauce over each chicken breast and top with a couple pieces of mozzarella. Cover the grill and cook for 3 to 4 minutes longer, until the cheese is melted and the chicken is cooked through. Serve hot.

grilled lamb chops MAKES 12 LAMB CHOPS

My favorite thing to cook on the beach is grilled lamb chops (also one of my favorite things to eat, come to think of it). Now, that may sound a bit odd at first, but think about it: They're small, they cook quickly, and they're easy to eat with your hands. Yeah, that's right, no need for a knife and fork here. Just grab one by the bone and go for it.

Grated zest of 1 lemon

Juice of 2 lemons

3 tablespoons olive oil

1 tablespoon chopped fresh oregano leaves

1/2 teaspoon garlic powder

Salt and freshly ground black pepper

12 lamb chops

In a large bowl, combine the lemon zest, lemon juice, oil, oregano, and garlic powder. Generously season each side of the lamb chops with salt and pepper. Add to the lemon juice mixture and toss to combine. Cover and refrigerate for 1 hour. Remove from the refrigerator about 20 minutes before cooking.

Preheat an outdoor grill to medium-high. Grill the lamb chops for 3 to 4 minutes, until slightly charred on one side. Flip and cook for 2 to 3 minutes longer for medium-rare to medium doneness. Serve hot.

grilled lamb chops:

perfect beach

food!

best barbecue ribs ever SERVES 6

The name pretty much says it all. These ribs are insanity.

¼ cup (55 g) brown sugar

2 tablespoons chili powder

1 tablespoon salt

1 teaspoon freshly ground black pepper

1 teaspoon dried oregano

½ teaspoon ground cayenne

½ teaspoon garlic powder

½ teaspoon onion powder

2 racks baby back ribs

1 cup (240 ml) low-sodium chicken broth

2 tablespoons apple cider vinegar

1 cup (240 ml) barbecue sauce

Combine the brown sugar, chili powder, salt, black pepper, oregano, cayenne, garlic powder, and onion powder in a small bowl and rub the mixture onto both sides of the ribs. Cover and refrigerate for 1 hour, or up to overnight.

Preheat the oven to 250°F (120°C).

In a roasting pan, combine the broth and vinegar. Add the ribs to the pan. Cover with foil and tightly seal. Bake for 2 ½ hours. Remove the ribs from the pan and place them on a platter. Pour the liquid from the pan into a saucepan and bring to a boil. Lower the heat to a simmer and cook until it's reduced by half. Add the barbecue sauce.

Preheat an outdoor grill to medium-high. Put the ribs on the grill and cook for about 5 minutes on each side, until browned and slightly charred. Cut the ribs between the bones and toss them in a large bowl with the sauce. Serve hot.

grilled hanger steaks with jalapeño butter SERVES 4-6

As with most foods, if it's good quality, you really don't need to do much to make it taste great. This sentiment is certainly true when it comes to steak. I generously season it with salt and pepper, grill it, and then add just a little something like a flavored butter to make it special. With hanger steak, I like this jalapeño butter, but you can make the butter with blue cheese, garlic, roasted red peppers, anchovies . . . you get the idea.

½ cup (1 stick/115 g) unsalted butter, at room temperature

½ jalapeño, minced

2 (1-pound/455-g) hanger steaks, trimmed

Salt and freshly ground black pepper

Canola oil

In a small bowl, use a fork to mash the butter and jalapeño together. Mold the butter into a log shape and wrap it in plastic wrap. Chill in the refrigerator for 1 hour, or until firm.

Preheat an outdoor grill to medium-high.

Generously season both sides of each steak with salt and pepper and drizzle with oil. Put the steaks on the grill and cook for 5 to 6 minutes on each side for medium-rare. Let the steak rest for a few minutes before serving. Slice the meat across the grain and top each serving with 1 tablespoon of the jalapeño butter.

middle eastern spiced spatchcocked chicken with harissa yogurt SERVES 2-4

Don't let the term *spatchcock* scare you. It's much easier than it sounds, and it will make cooking a whole chicken on the grill faster and yield a tasty, juicy bird. As for the spices and the harissa yogurt? *Yum.* Harissa is widely available these days, but if you can't find it, just mix some garlic and hot pepper into your yogurt.

1   whole (3- to 4-pound/1.4- to 1.8-kg) chicken

2   tablespoons chili powder

1   tablespoon salt

1   teaspoon ground cinnamon

1   teaspoon garlic powder

½   teaspoon freshly ground black pepper

2   tablespoons canola oil

1   cup (240 ml) plain Greek yogurt

2   tablespoons harissa

1   tablespoon honey

Preheat an outdoor grill to medium-high.

To spatchcock the chicken, remove and discard the giblets. Place the chicken on a cutting board, breast side down. Use kitchen shears to cut along each side of the backbone to remove it. Trim off any excess fat. Flip the chicken breast side up, and firmly press down on each breast to break the bone and flatten the bird.

In a small bowl, combine the chili powder, salt, cinnamon, garlic powder, and pepper. Season both sides of the chicken with the spice mixture. Use a pastry brush to brush the chicken with the oil.

Place the chicken skin side down on the grill. Cover the grill and cook for 10 minutes. Flip the chicken and move it to a medium-low heat spot on the grill (or lower the temperature if using gas). Cover and cook for 10 minutes. Flip the chicken again and cook for 10 minutes, then flip one more time and cook for 10 minutes longer, or until the chicken reaches an internal temperature of 165°F (74°C). Remove to a carving board, tent with foil, and let stand for 5 minutes. Cut into pieces (it will be falling apart by this time).

In a small bowl, combine the yogurt, harissa, and honey. Serve with the chicken.

spiced duck breasts with balsamic blackberry sauce SERVES 8

Long Island is famous for a lot of things, and one of them is duck. In fact, the most popular species of duck in the United States is White Pekin, also known as Long Island duck. In the town of Flanders, there is a giant white duck monument that a farmer built in 1931. It is now a museum and one of the "Seven Wonders of Long Island." (I'm not making this up.)

Since this cookbook is filled with recipes inspired by my home, it is only fitting to have at least one duck recipe. Duck is on the fatty side, and I think it really benefits from an acidic element like vinegar and tart-sweet fruit. Reducing the balsamic vinegar gives it a sweetness, but it still has that tart bite to it.

1   cup (240 ml) balsamic vinegar

1   quart (670 g) blackberries

    Salt and freshly ground black pepper

8   (6-ounce/170-g) boneless duck breast halves, with skin

1   tablespoon chili powder

1 1/2   teaspoons ground coriander

1   teaspoon ground cumin

1   teaspoon dry mustard

In a medium nonreactive saucepan, boil the vinegar over high heat until it is reduced by half, about 7 minutes. Add the blackberries and cook, stirring very gently, until they are just softened, about 2 minutes. Using a slotted spoon, transfer the blackberries to a bowl. Boil the liquid over high heat until it is reduced to 1/3 cup (75 ml), about 3 minutes. Carefully pour the accumulated juices from the blackberry bowl into the saucepan and boil for about 30 seconds longer. Season the reduction with salt and pepper to taste and pour it over the blackberries. Set aside.

Preheat an outdoor grill or a grill pan to medium.

Using a sharp knife, score the duck skin in a crosshatch pattern, taking care not to cut into the flesh itself. In a small bowl, combine the chili powder, coriander, cumin, and mustard. Season the duck breasts with salt and pepper and rub the spice mixture into the skin. Grill the duck breasts skin side down until lightly charred and crisp, about 3 minutes. Turn the breasts and cook for 5 to 6 minutes longer for medium doneness. Transfer the duck to a carving board, tent with aluminum foil, and let rest for 5 minutes.

Thinly slice the duck breasts on the diagonal and transfer to plates. Serve the duck with the blackberry sauce.

if you aren't a fan of duck, try this recipe with pork chops.

hoisin ginger pork chops SERVES 4

Hoisin sauce is like a Chinese barbecue sauce and goes perfectly with pork. It is made of fermented soybeans and has the salty-sweet thing going on. This mixture of hoisin sauce with soy sauce, ginger, garlic, and sesame oil is pretty universal and can be used on chicken, shrimp kebabs, ribs, you name it.

4   center-cut, bone-in pork chops, 1 1/2 to 2 inches (4 to 5 cm) thick

Salt and freshly ground black pepper

1/4   cup (60 ml) hoisin sauce

2   tablespoons soy sauce

2   tablespoons grated peeled ginger

2   cloves garlic, grated

2   teaspoons toasted sesame oil

Preheat an outdoor grill to medium.

Generously season each side of the pork chops with salt and pepper. In a bowl, combine the hoisin sauce, soy sauce, ginger, garlic, and sesame oil.

Place the pork chops on the grill and cover the grill. Cook for 4 minutes. Flip the chops, brush with the hoisin sauce mixture, then cover the grill and cook for 4 minutes. Flip and brush again, then cover and cook for 2 minutes. Flip and baste, then cover and cook for 2 minutes longer.

Remove the chops from the grill, tent with foil, and let stand for 5 minutes. Serve hot.

skillet paella SERVES 4

I have this fantasy of building a fire in the yard and making a huge traditional paella, then carrying it to the table and serving it family style. I usually make mine in a skillet, which works perfectly well, but if you have a paella pan, go for it!

1	tablespoon extra-virgin olive oil
2	(6-inch/15-cm) fresh chorizo links (about 6 ounces/170 g total), diced
3	large boneless, skinless chicken thighs (12 ounces/340 g total), cut into 1-inch (2.5-cm) chunks
	Salt and freshly ground black pepper
1	yellow onion, chopped
1	red bell pepper, cored, cut in half, and thinly sliced lengthwise
2	cloves garlic, minced
1 ½	teaspoons paprika
¾	teaspoon dried thyme
1	bay leaf
1 ½	cups (300 g) short-grain white rice, such as Arborio
1	(14-ounce/400-g) can whole peeled tomatoes, with their juice, crushed with your hands
3	cups (700 ml) low-sodium chicken stock
½	cup (60 g) frozen peas
8	ounces (225 g) medium shrimp, peeled and deveined
4	scallions, white and green parts, thinly sliced
	Lemon wedges for serving

In a large (12- to 14-inch/30.5- to 35.5-cm), deep, straight-sided skillet, heat the oil over medium-high heat. Add the chorizo and cook, stirring, until the fat renders and the sausage begins to brown, about 5 minutes. Transfer to a paper towel–lined plate.

Season the chicken with salt and black pepper and add it to the skillet. Cook, stirring occasionally, until evenly browned, 6 to 7 minutes. Remove the chicken from the pan to the plate with the chorizo and reduce the heat to medium. Add the onion and bell pepper to the skillet and cook, stirring, until softened, about 5 minutes. Add the garlic and cook for 1 minute. Add the paprika, thyme, and bay leaf and stir for 1 minute to toast the spices. Add the rice and cook, stirring constantly, until the rice is coated, about 1 minute. Add the tomatoes and juice, stir, and cook until the liquid is absorbed, about 5 minutes.

Add the stock, ½ teaspoon salt, ½ teaspoon black pepper, the chorizo, and chicken to the pan and bring to a boil. Reduce the heat to maintain a low simmer, cover, and cook for 20 minutes. Scatter the peas and shrimp over the top of the paella (do not stir). If the rice looks dry, drizzle a little water or stock over the top. Cover and cook just until the shrimp turn pink and the peas are cooked through, 3 to 4 minutes more.

Scatter the scallions over the top and serve the paella family style with lemon wedges for squeezing over the top.

chili-honey-
garlic shrimp
kebab

swordfish
kebabs
with
mint pesto

tzatziki

jerked beef kebabs

mediterranean chicken kebabs

chili-honey-garlic shrimp kebabs

MAKES 4-5 KEBABS

Spicy, sweet, and savory: what a combo. My friend Keith loves grilled shrimp, so I like to make this dish for him, and I serve it with steamed rice or add it to a salad.

2	pounds (910 g; 16- to 20-count) shrimp
	Salt and freshly ground black pepper
1	tablespoon olive oil
1/3	cup (75 ml) honey
2	tablespoons chili garlic sauce

Soak 8 to 10 wooden skewers in water for at least 30 minutes.

Preheat an outdoor grill to medium-high. Make sure the grates are clean.

Thread the shrimp onto the skewers, using two skewers for each kebab so that they hold securely and are easy to flip while cooking. Use 4 or 5 shrimp per kebab. Season both sides of each kebab with salt and pepper. Use a pastry brush to coat each side with oil.

In a small microwave-safe bowl, combine the honey and chili garlic sauce. Microwave for 20 to 30 seconds (or heat the mixture in a small saucepan to liquefy the honey) and whisk to combine.

Place the kebabs on the grill. Cover the grill and cook for about 2 minutes, until the shrimp begin to turn pink. Flip and brush with the honey mixture. Cook for 1 minute. Flip and brush the other side with the honey mixture. Cook for 1 minute. Flip again and brush with more sauce. Flip and brush again. Serve hot.

jerked beef kebabs

MAKES 12 KEBABS

In St. Bart's, there is a restaurant called Meat and Potatoes, and you'll never guess what they serve. It is a small, funky, open-air space, run by young, good-looking Frenchies, across from a salt marsh near Grand Saline beach. Their specialty is steaks, of course, many that look fit for Fred Flinstone, but my favorite is their kebabs—beef, chicken, and shrimp. This recipe is my best attempt at making something close to theirs. Serve them with—you guessed it—potatoes.

1 1/4	pounds (570 g) top sirloin steak, cut into 1-inch (2.5-cm) chunks
4	scallions, white and green parts, chopped
1/2	small jalapeño, chopped, including seeds (add more if you want it spicier)
2	cloves garlic, smashed
	Juice of 1 lime
1	tablespoon olive oil
1	teaspoon light brown sugar
1/2	teaspoon dried thyme
1/2	teaspoon ground allspice
	Pinch of ground cloves
	Pinch of ground cinnamon
	Salt and freshly ground black pepper

Put the beef in a nonreactive bowl. Put the scallions, jalapeño, and garlic in a small food processor and pulse until finely chopped. Add the lime juice, oil, brown sugar, thyme, allspice, cloves, and cinnamon and puree until a smooth paste forms. Add the mixture to the beef along with a pinch each of salt and pepper, and toss until the meat is thoroughly coated. Cover and refrigerate for 1 hour.

Soak twelve 8-inch (20-cm) wooden skewers in water for at least 30 minutes. Remove the meat from the fridge and let stand for 10 to 15 minutes. Skewer 3 or 4 chunks of meat onto each skewer.

Preheat an outdoor grill to high. Brush the grill grates with an oil-soaked towel and grill the kebabs, turning once, until medium-rare, about 2 minutes per side. Serve hot.

swordfish kebabs with mint pesto

MAKES 8 KEBABS

If the idea of grilling fish intimidates you, try this recipe. Kebabs are a much less intimidating way to wade into the waters of seafood grilling, and swordfish is hearty and holds up on a metal grate. You'll notice that the fish is cut into slightly larger cubes than in my other kebab recipes, so it doesn't dry out on the grill but instead stays nice and juicy. If you can't find swordfish, try using salmon or tuna. The mint pesto tastes so refreshing and bright, and you can toss the leftovers with rice, couscous, or orzo pasta for a side dish.

1¼	pounds (570 g) swordfish steak, cut into 1½-inch (4-cm) cubes
¼	cup (20 g) sliced almonds
1	large clove garlic, smashed
1	cup (40 g) packed fresh mint leaves
¼	cup (10 g) packed flat-leaf parsley leaves
	Grated zest of 1 lemon
5	tablespoons (75 ml) extra-virgin olive oil
	Salt and freshly ground black pepper
	Pinch of red chile flakes (optional)

Put the fish cubes in a bowl. Soak eight 8-inch (20-cm) wooden skewers in water for at least 30 minutes.

Meanwhile, to make the pesto, put the almonds and garlic in a food processor and pulse until finely chopped. Add the mint, parsley, and lemon zest and pulse until finely ground. Transfer the mixture to a small bowl and whisk in the oil. Season the pesto with salt and pepper to taste and the chile flakes, if using. Pour about one-third of the pesto over the swordfish and toss to evenly coat. Reserve the remaining pesto for serving. Refrigerate for at least 30 minutes and up to 4 hours.

Preheat an outdoor grill to medium-high.

Skewer 3 or 4 chunks of swordfish on each skewer and grill, turning once, until just cooked through, 2 to 3 minutes per side. Serve the skewers with additional pesto drizzled over the top.

mediterranean chicken kebabs with pita and tzatziki

MAKES 12 KEBABS

Ahhh, I could eat this whole recipe all by myself. Every summer in Southampton, the Greek Orthodox church has a big Greek festival. They have dancers in traditional costumes, children sing, there are games, and there is a *ton* of food. The braised lamb shanks are exceptional, and even though it's summertime, when it seems like braised lamb shank would be too heavy, I find a way. They also serve chicken souvlaki that is totally craveable, so I came up with this recipe to satisfy my hunger the other fifty-one weeks of the year.

¼ cup (60 ml) extra-virgin olive oil

Juice of 1 lemon

4 garlic cloves, smashed

¾ teaspoon dried oregano

1¼ pounds (570 g) boneless, skinless chicken breast, cut into 1-inch (2.5-cm) cubes

Salt and freshly ground black pepper

Pita bread rounds

Tzatziki sauce

Lettuce leaves

Crumbled feta cheese

Diced tomatoes

Za'atar spice blend

In a large nonreactive bowl, whisk the oil, lemon juice, garlic, and oregano until combined. Stir in the chicken pieces, season with salt and pepper, and refrigerate for about 15 minutes and no longer than 30 minutes.

Soak twelve 8-inch (20-cm) wooden skewers in water for at least 30 minutes. Preheat an outdoor grill to medium-high.

Skewer 3 or 4 cubes of chicken onto each skewer. Using a pastry brush, brush each kebab with any oil left in the bowl of marinade to coat. Grill the skewers, turning once, until cooked through, 3 to 4 minutes per side. To serve, spread tzatziki on a pita and line it with a lettuce leaf. Lay 2 or 3 skewers on top of the lettuce, and holding the pita in your hand and closing it around the meat, remove the skewers. Scatter cheese and tomatoes over the meat and garnish with a dusting of za'atar. Serve immediately.

how cute is Fionula??

roasted halibut with tomato-caper relish SERVES 6-8

When I have a group over for dinner and I don't have much time to cook but I still want to make something that looks impressive, I cook a large piece of fish and serve it family style. On a big platter, it looks much more dramatic than individual pieces of fish. Everyone takes as much or as little as they want. I made this halibut a couple of summers ago for my friend Mark's birthday party; it was an instant hit and has become a regular on my party menus. I usually buy the fish with the skin on, as it helps hold it together when people serve themselves, but you certainly can get it without.

1 (2- to 3-pound/.9- to 1.4-kg) piece center-cut halibut fillet, bones removed

  Extra-virgin olive oil

1 lemon, zested and halved

  Salt and freshly ground black pepper

1 pint (280 g) grape tomatoes, quartered

1 small shallot, finely chopped

2 tablespoons brined capers, drained, brine reserved

1 teaspoon red wine vinegar

12 fresh basil leaves, torn

Preheat the oven to 400°F (205°C). Oil a baking dish.

Set the fish in the dish and rub the surface all over with oil. Squeeze the juice of half of the lemon over it and season it well with salt and pepper. Roast until cooked through but still moist, 15 to 20 minutes.

Meanwhile, put the lemon zest, 2 teaspoons lemon juice, the tomatoes, shallot, capers, vinegar, and 1 tablespoon oil in a small bowl and toss well to combine. Season the relish with salt and pepper to taste and mix well. Taste and add a little of the caper brine or a bit more lemon juice if it needs more flavor; fold in the basil.

Remove the fish from the oven and immediately scatter the tomato relish over the top while the fish is still hot. Serve family style at the table.

vegetable manicotti SERVES 4-6

My mom always made the best manicotti when I was a kid. Her recipe was really simple: a ricotta filling, tomato sauce, and melted cheese. I loved it. Come to think of it, she hasn't made it in years. Manicotti can sound like a heavy meal, but this recipe is light and summery. It doesn't have any mozzarella in the filling, and it has more veggies than cheese, so it's less heavy. You can substitute other vegetables like cooked broccoli or cooked drained spinach if you like. This dish is perfect to take to a summer potluck.

For the filling:

- 1   tablespoon extra-virgin olive oil
- 1   large yellow onion, chopped
- 2   small cloves garlic, minced
- 1   small zucchini (about 4 ounces/115 g total), finely diced
- 1   small yellow squash (about 4 ounces/115 g total), finely diced

    Salt and freshly ground black pepper

- 1   (15-ounce/425-g) container whole-milk ricotta
- ½   cup (60 g) finely grated Parmesan cheese
- 1   large egg, beaten
- 3   tablespoons chopped fresh flat-leaf parsley leaves

For the tomato sauce:

- 1   (28-ounce/794-g) can whole peeled San Marzano tomatoes
- 1   teaspoon salt
- ¼   teaspoon freshly ground black pepper
- ¼   cup (25 g) chopped fresh basil leaves

For the manicotti:

- 12 manicotti shells, cooked according to the package instructions and drained
- ¼   cup (30 g) grated Parmesan cheese

    Torn fresh basil leaves (optional)

Start the filling: Heat the oil in a large skillet over medium heat. Add the onion and garlic and cook until softened, about 4 minutes. Add the zucchini and yellow squash, season with salt and pepper, and cook, stirring frequently, until the squash softens but is not mushy, about 4 more minutes. Pour the mixture into a bowl and let stand until cool.

Make the sauce: Put the tomatoes in a food processor and pulse until coarsely ground (or chop the tomatoes by hand). Transfer to a bowl, add the salt and pepper and stir in the basil.

Preheat the oven to 375°F (190°C). Oil a 9-by-13-inch (23-by-33-cm) baking dish.

Finish the filling and assemble the manicotti: Put the ricotta, the ½ cup (60 g) Parmesan, ½ teaspoon salt, and pepper to taste in a medium bowl. Add the egg and stir to combine. Fold in the cooled vegetables and the parsley and stir until combined. Transfer the filling to a large resealable plastic bag. Snip a large hole out of one corner of the bag with scissors and use the bag to fill the cooked manicotti tubes.

Spread about 1 cup (240 ml) of the tomato sauce in the bottom of the baking dish and arrange the filled manicotti on top. Spread the remaining sauce over the pasta, sprinkle the ¼ cup (30 g) Parmesan over the top, and bake until the filling is set and the sauce is bubbling, about 40 minutes. Let stand for 10 minutes, scatter the basil over the top, if using, and serve.

crowd pleaser!

west virginia–style hot dogs

SERVES 8-10

It seems every area of the country has its own way of dressing hot dogs. I like New York–style with the sauerkraut and mustard just fine, and Chicago dogs are pretty good, too, but nothing beats a West Virginia dog. We make ours with chili sauce, yellow mustard, and coleslaw. The mayonnaise of the slaw next to the spice of the chili and the tang of the mustard is pure perfection. I like to make these on a day when we're all hanging by the pool. I put the chili on the stove or in a slow cooker and just let everybody go in and serve themselves as they get hungry. It's a paper plate and potato chip kind of day, totally easy, laid-back, and *fun*.

For the chili sauce:

- 2 pounds (910 g) lean ground beef
- 1 yellow onion, grated
- 1 (16-ounce/454-g) can tomato sauce
- 1 (12-ounce/340-g) can tomato paste
- 2 tablespoons chili powder
- 2 tablespoons sugar
- 1½ teaspoons salt
- 1 teaspoon freshly ground black pepper
- 1 teaspoon garlic salt
- 2 bay leaves
- 1 tablespoon white wine vinegar

For serving:

Good-quality hot dogs, grilled, steamed, or boiled

Hot dog buns

Yellow mustard

Coleslaw (your favorite recipe or store-bought)

Make the chili sauce: In a stockpot or Dutch oven, combine the beef (do not brown first), onion, tomato sauce, tomato paste, chili powder, sugar, salt, pepper, garlic salt, and 2 cups (480 ml) water. Stir until combined, then add the bay leaves. Cover and simmer over medium-low heat for about 2 hours.

Stir in the vinegar and simmer for 30 minutes longer.

Place your hot dogs on buns and top with chili sauce, yellow mustard, and coleslaw.

This makes a good amount of chili, so plan on leftovers or freezing the leftovers if you don't have a big group.

pool
party!

side

I swear I could make a whole meal on sides alone. So many times, I'll look at a restaurant menu and I'll just want to order appetizers and side dishes, forgoing the entrée all together. There is just so much you can do with vegetables and grains, especially in the summer when everything is at its peak. Many of the recipes in this chapter were created after visits to the Green Thumb market, where I shop nearly every day to pick up whatever looks best. I'll get home with my bounty and ask myself, "OK, what now?" and cook up something good. The beauty of summer vegetables is that they're so good on their own, you don't have to do much. Sometimes just a ripe tomato, sliced with a drizzle of olive oil and a sprinkle of flaky sea salt, is all you need for the perfect side.

corn pudding SERVES 6

Corn pudding is like soft, creamy, decadent cornbread eaten with a spoon.

2	cups (480 ml) milk
½	cup (120 ml) heavy cream
4	ears corn, husked
1	tablespoon extra-virgin olive oil
1	sweet onion, finely chopped
½	cup (1 stick/115 g) unsalted butter
½	cup (70 g) cornmeal
6	large eggs, separated
3	ounces (85 g) sharp cheddar cheese, shredded (about 1 cup)
1	teaspoon plus a pinch of salt
½	teaspoon freshly ground black pepper

Preheat the oven to 350°F (175°C). Butter a 10-by-15-inch (25-by-38-cm) baking dish.

In a large saucepan, bring the milk and cream to a simmer over medium heat. Add the corn, cover, and cook over medium-low heat, turning a few times, until tender, about 10 minutes.

Meanwhile, in a medium skillet, heat the oil over medium heat. Add the onion and cook until softened, about 8 minutes.

Transfer the corn to a plate and let cool. Remove the saucepan from the heat and swirl in the butter until melted. Let cool to room temperature.

Cut the corn kernels off the cobs and add them to the saucepan, then add the onion. Whisk in the cornmeal, egg yolks, cheese, the 1 teaspoon salt, and the pepper.

In a large stainless-steel bowl, beat the egg whites with the pinch of salt at high speed until firm peaks form. Fold the whites into the corn mixture and pour into the prepared baking dish. Bake for about 30 minutes, until the corn pudding is puffed and golden brown. Let the pudding rest for about 5 minutes before serving.

apricot herb couscous SERVES 4-6

A few years ago, on a trip to Morocco, I had a couscous similar to this but made with dried apricots. Since apricots are in the height of their season during summer, I like making it with fresh ones, but you could certainly use dried if you wish. This is a really speedy side dish to put together.

1	(10-ounce/283-g) box couscous
¼	cup (25 g) minced fresh flat-leaf parsley
¼	cup (40 g) diced fresh or dried apricots
¼	cup (20 g) sliced almonds
2	tablespoons extra-virgin olive oil
1	tablespoon fresh lemon juice
	Salt and freshly ground black pepper

Cook the couscous according to the package instructions. Use a fork to fluff and fold in the parsley, apricots, almonds, oil, and lemon juice. Season with salt and pepper to taste and serve hot.

a speedy side!

all-american potato salad

SERVES 6-8

I love a simple potato salad. I don't put much in mine other than mayo, mustard, and herbs.

3 pounds (1.4 kg) whole small round potatoes

Salt

¼ cup (60 ml) mayonnaise

¼ cup (25 g) chopped scallions, white and green parts

1 tablespoon Dijon mustard

1 tablespoon minced fresh tarragon

1 tablespoon minced fresh flat-leaf parsley

Juice of 1 lemon (about 3 tablespoons)

¼ teaspoon freshly ground black pepper

Fresh cilantro leaves

Put the potatoes in a large pot and cover with salted water. Bring to a boil, reduce the heat to a simmer, cover, and cook until fork tender, about 30 minutes. Drain and let cool completely. Slice the potatoes about ¼ inch (6 mm) thick.

In a large bowl, combine the mayonnaise, scallions, mustard, tarragon, parsley, lemon juice, 1 teaspoon salt, and the pepper. Add the potatoes and toss gently to combine. Cover and chill in the refrigerator until serving time. Serve cold, garnished with cilantro.

bourbon bacon slaw

SERVES 4-6

Oh hey, y'all. Yep, this recipe has mayonnaise, bourbon, *and* bacon.

½ cup (120 ml) mayonnaise

2 tablespoons bourbon

2 tablespoons brown sugar

1 tablespoon Dijon mustard

2 teaspoons chili powder

1 teaspoon salt

½ teaspoon garlic powder

¼ teaspoon freshly ground black pepper

Juice of 1 lime

1 medium head purple cabbage, cored and thinly sliced

8 slices bacon, chopped, cooked until crispy, and drained on paper towels

In a small bowl, combine the mayonnaise, bourbon, brown sugar, mustard, chili powder, salt, garlic powder, pepper, and lime juice until well combined. Pour the dressing over the cabbage in a large bowl and toss to coat. Just before serving, stir in the bacon.

great on a sandwich or taco

zucchini and squash bake SERVES 4-6

I made this side dish once when I realized it was almost time to serve dinner to my guests and I'd forgotten to make any vegetables. I looked around the kitchen and saw that I had some extra squash and zucchini, so I quickly sliced it up, tossed it with a little oil, and sprinkled it with some seasoned bread crumbs and Parmesan. No one had any idea that it was a last-minute throw-together, and almost everyone had seconds.

2	zucchinis, thinly sliced
2	yellow squash, thinly sliced
2	tablespoons extra-virgin olive oil
½	teaspoon salt
2	cups (230 g) bread crumbs
½	teaspoon garlic salt
1	teaspoon dried oregano
2	tablespoons grated Parmesan cheese
2	tablespoons unsalted butter, melted

Preheat the oven to 400°F (205°C). Oil or butter an 8-inch (20-cm) square baking dish.

In a large bowl, toss the zucchini and squash with the oil and salt. Place in the baking dish.

In a small bowl, combine the bread crumbs with the garlic salt, oregano, Parmesan, and butter. Sprinkle the bread crumb mixture over the zucchini and squash. Bake for 30 minutes, or until golden brown. Serve hot.

quinoa tabbouleh SERVES 6-8

Tabbouleh is a Middle Eastern salad that is typically made with bulgur wheat.
On a trip to Israel, I ate it almost every single day. I am borderline obsessed with
quinoa, so a few summers ago, I decided to swap it in for the bulgur. The results?
Glorious! Quinoa tabbouleh has since become a staple on my summer menu;
my friends ask for it when they come to my house, and they also ask me to bring
some along when I visit them. If I'm picnicking, I pack it up in individual-serving-size
Chinese take-out containers.

2	cups (340 g) quinoa, well rinsed
1	English cucumber, peeled and diced
1	pint (280 g) grape tomatoes, halved
1	bunch scallions, white parts only, thinly sliced
¼	cup (25 g) minced fresh mint
¼	cup (25 g) minced fresh flat-leaf parsley
½	cup (120 ml) extra-virgin olive oil
	Juice of 1 lemon
1	teaspoon salt
¼	teaspoon freshly ground black pepper

In a medium saucepan, bring 4 cups
(960 ml) water and the quinoa to a boil.
Reduce the heat to a simmer, cover, and
cook for 20 minutes, or until all the water
is absorbed. Fluff with a fork. Transfer
the quinoa to a large bowl and let cool
completely.

Add the cucumber, tomatoes, scallions,
mint, and parsley to the quinoa and stir
to combine. In a small bowl, whisk the oil,
lemon juice, salt, and pepper together. Add
to the quinoa mixture and toss to combine.
Serve at room temperature.

old-school spinach-stuffed tomatoes MAKES 6 STUFFED TOMATOES

If you've ever been to Joe's Stone Crab in Miami Beach, you've probably ordered the stuffed tomatoes. They are so freaking good! The portions are really big, so I usually end up taking some home; I chop up the leftovers and add them to my scrambled eggs in the morning. Yum. Joe's puts American cheese on top of theirs, but I like using Gruyère. Honestly, though, it's melted cheese, so obviously it tastes great and you can use whatever kind you prefer.

6	medium round tomatoes
1	(9-ounce/255-g) bag baby spinach, steamed, cooled, and squeezed of any liquid
¼	cup (60 ml) sour cream or plain Greek yogurt
2	tablespoons grated Parmesan cheese
	Pinch of sea salt
¼	teaspoon freshly ground black pepper
¾	cup (90 g) grated Gruyère cheese

Preheat the oven to 400°F (205°C).

Use a serrated knife to cut the top off of each tomato. Use a grapefruit knife (or a paring knife) to cut out the inside of the tomato. You may need to use your fingers to pull it out after cutting. With a spoon, remove any leftover seeds or pulp.

In a blender or food processor, puree the spinach, sour cream, Parmesan, salt, and pepper. Gently spoon the mixture into each tomato and top with Gruyère. Place the tomatoes in a baking dish and bake for 20 to 25 minutes, until the cheese is melted and bubbly. Serve hot.

green beans with olive-almond tapenade SERVES 4-6

I *looooove* green olives. I think green olives are the sole reason I like a dirty martini. (I order mine extra dirty—so dirty it's cloudy. Then the next day none of my rings fit.) Turns out, that briny green flavor pairs just as nicely with green beans as it does with vodka. This dish is good served either warm or cold, and it's great for a picnic. You can use as much or as little of the tapenade as you like—the leftovers will keep for a while in the fridge, and it'd be great spread on crostini or mixed with mayo and spread on bread for sandwiches.

¼	cup (35 g) whole almonds, toasted
½	cup (90 g) large pitted green olives
	Grated zest of ½ lemon
3	tablespoons flat-leaf parsley leaves, plus a little more for garnish
2	tablespoons extra-virgin olive oil
	Salt and freshly ground black pepper
1 ½	pounds (680 g) green beans, trimmed and halved crosswise

Put the almonds in a food processor and pulse until finely chopped. Add the olives, lemon zest, and parsley and pulse until finely ground and the mixture is a thick paste. Add the oil and pulse until combined and emulsified; season with salt and pepper to taste.

Bring a large pot of water to a boil and salt it generously. Add the green beans and cook until crisp-tender, about 4 minutes. Drain and transfer to a serving bowl.

Add the tapenade to the beans and toss until evenly coated. Serve warm or at room temperature, garnished with chopped parsley.

roasted spaghetti squash with curry-shallot butter SERVES 4-6

Some people turn their noses up at the flavor of curry, but I think they just haven't had good curry. Another food besides curry that I love? Spaghetti squash. Did you know that a cup of spaghetti squash has only 42 calories? Hello, it's bikini season and I can eat mass quantities.

1   spaghetti squash, about 2½ pounds (1.2 kg)

4   tablespoons (½ stick/55 g) unsalted butter, at room temperature

2   teaspoons mild curry powder

2   teaspoons minced shallot

1   teaspoon minced fresh cilantro

Finely grated zest of ½ lemon

½   teaspoon salt, plus more if needed

Freshly ground black pepper

⅓   cup (40 g) toasted pine nuts

Preheat the oven to 400°F (205°C). Line a baking sheet with parchment paper.

With a sharp knife, carefully cut about four ½-inch (12-mm) slits in the squash to allow steam to escape while it cooks. Put the squash on the prepared baking sheet and roast for about 1 ½ hours. Let the squash cool for about 20 minutes on the baking sheet.

Meanwhile, in a small bowl, with a fork, mash the butter, curry powder, shallot, cilantro, lemon zest, salt, and pepper to taste until well combined.

Cut the squash in half and use a spoon to scoop out the seeds. With a large fork, pull the squash fibers away from the outer peel (use a towel to hold the squash in place if necessary). Transfer the warm squash to a serving bowl and top it with the curry butter. Toss until the butter is melted and evenly mixed. Taste and season with more salt and pepper if necessary. Serve warm with the pine nuts scattered on top.

moroccan carrots SERVES 4

I traveled through Morocco a few years ago and came home with caftans, tablecloths, tagines, embroidered blankets, and about five extra pounds. The food was so good. *So good.* (Though by the end of the trip, I needed a nice long break from couscous.) At lunch and dinner, an array of salads would be brought out and placed on the table. I would stuff my face until I was totally full, and then the main course would come. At every restaurant, there was a carrot salad that was pretty consistent from place to place. The flavors of the spices drove me wild! (I know, it's a salad. But hey, I like salads.) The key here is to cut the carrots very thin, and to know that the salad gets better the longer it sits as the carrots soak up the dressing and begin to soften.

3	large carrots, peeled
1/2	teaspoon ground cumin
1/2	teaspoon sweet paprika
	Pinch of ground cinnamon
	Pinch of ground cayenne
2	tablespoons extra-virgin olive oil
1	tablespoon fresh lemon juice
1	small clove garlic, grated or very finely minced
1/2	cup (20 g) packed fresh flat-leaf parsley leaves, roughly chopped
	Salt and freshly ground black pepper
	Harissa

Using a mandoline slicer or very sharp knife, very thinly slice the carrots on the diagonal about 1/16 inch (2 mm) thick and put them in a bowl.

Put the cumin, paprika, cinnamon, and cayenne in a small dry skillet over medium-low heat. Cook, stirring frequently, until the spices are fragrant, about 1 minute. Add the oil and swirl the pan to mix. Add the lemon juice and swirl the pan; when the mixture begins to bubble, add the garlic and cook, swirling the pan, for 15 to 20 seconds, until the dressing is very hot. Pour the hot dressing over the carrots and toss with a large rubber spatula until the carrots are evenly coated and have absorbed the dressing. Add the parsley, season with salt and pepper, and toss until combined.

Serve at room temperature, with harissa, or refrigerate until ready to serve.

lemony brown rice with cucumber and feta SERVES 4-6

As you've probably gathered, when I'm having friends over for dinner I like recipes that I can make ahead of time. This brown rice is best served at room temperature or cold, so it's ideal to make in advance and pull out when it's time to sit down for dinner. It tastes really fresh and bright, and the cucumbers are especially nice when it's hot outside. I love this served with grilled salmon.

3 cups (585 g) cooked, cooled brown rice

1 (6-inch/15-cm) seedless cucumber or ½ English cucumber, diced

4 ounces (115 g) feta cheese, crumbled

½ cup (20 g) coarsely chopped fresh dill

Finely grated zest of 1 lemon

2 tablespoons fresh lemon juice

1 teaspoon Dijon mustard

1 teaspoon honey

3 tablespoons extra-virgin olive oil

Salt and freshly ground black pepper

Put the rice, cucumber, cheese, and dill in a medium bowl and toss until combined.

In a small bowl, whisk the lemon zest and juice, the mustard, and honey together until combined. While whisking, slowly add the oil and whisk until thick and emulsified; season with salt and pepper to taste.

Pour the dressing over the rice mixture and toss until evenly combined and the dressing is absorbed. Taste and adjust the seasoning with salt and pepper if necessary. Serve immediately or refrigerate until ready to serve.

lemon mint baby zucchini SERVES 4-6

I used to have zucchini in my garden, and it would grow like a weed. One day the vegetable would look normal and the next it would be gigantic. If you can get it when it is still small, it is much more tender. Many farmers' markets and grocery stores are selling the baby version these days, and it is quite easy to prepare and makes for a nice presentation. If you can't get the baby variety, just cut a regular zucchini into matchstick pieces. Lemon and mint are my favorite seasonings for zucchini.

3   tablespoons extra-virgin olive oil

1   large clove garlic, minced

3   pounds (1.4 kg) baby zucchini, trimmed and halved lengthwise

Salt and freshly ground black pepper

3   tablespoons fresh lemon juice

½   cup (30 g) chopped fresh mint

In a large skillet, heat the oil over medium heat. Add the garlic and cook until fragrant but not browned, about 30 seconds. Increase the heat to medium-high, add the zucchini, season with salt and pepper, and cook, stirring occasionally, until crisp-tender, about 8 minutes. Add the lemon juice and transfer the zucchini to a bowl. Stir in the mint. Serve hot or at room temperature.

green and wax bean salad

This is a recipe I developed for *The Kitchen*. Each of the co-hosts were to give a different spin on green beans, and I was tasked with a salad. Usually, if I make a green bean salad, I do it with some orange segments, cherry tomatoes, and sesame vinaigrette, but the day before I had made a kale salad with blue cheese and bacon. I tried the same thing with green and yellow beans, and it was delicious! I wanted to keep the recipe on the lighter side, so I used turkey bacon (I had also just returned from a trip to LA, where every salad I ordered came with turkey bacon—go figure), but you could certainly use regular pork bacon.

8	ounces (225 g) green beans
8	ounces (225 g) yellow wax beans
4	ounces (115 g) blue cheese (or goat cheese), crumbled
¼	cup (40 g) dried cranberries
¼	cup (25 g) candied walnuts
1	tablespoon minced fresh chives
6	slices turkey bacon, cooked, cooled, and cut into ¼-inch (6-mm) pieces
1	tablespoon Dijon mustard
1	tablespoon white wine vinegar or Champagne vinegar
1	shallot, minced
3	tablespoons extra-virgin olive oil
	Salt and freshly ground black pepper

Bring a pot of water to a boil. Prepare an ice-water bath. Blanch the green beans until crisp-tender. Immediately transfer to the ice water to stop the cooking. Repeat with the wax beans. Drain the blanched beans thoroughly.

In a large bowl, combine the beans, cheese, cranberries, walnuts, chives, and bacon.

In a small bowl, whisk together the mustard and vinegar. Add the shallot. Whisk in the oil until emulsified. Season with salt and pepper to taste.

Add the dressing to the salad and toss to coat. Season with more pepper and serve at room temperature.

green goddess corn on the cob

SERVES 8

I have one word for this recipe: *tasty*. I am crazy about green goddess dressing, and I love it on corn just as much as on salads. Many of us have had chili powder and cheese on corn, so I wanted to give the same concept a new twist with the goddess dressing as inspiration. Don't be turned off by anchovies; they are the key to reaching that umami flavor nirvana. In this recipe, I simmer the corn, but you can absolutely put this on grilled corn. If you have any leftover spread, put it in a tomato sandwich or use as a dip for crudités.

8	ears sweet corn, husked
½	cup (20 g) loosely packed fresh basil leaves
¼	cup (10 g) fresh flat-leaf parsley leaves
4	scallions, green parts only, coarsely chopped
2	oil-packed anchovy fillets, drained
¼	cup (30 g) finely grated Parmesan cheese, plus more for serving
½	cup (120 ml) mayonnaise
	Freshly ground black pepper

Bring a large stockpot of water to a boil over high heat. Add the corn, reduce the heat to medium-low, cover, and simmer until the corn is cooked through and tender, about 5 minutes. Drain.

Meanwhile, put the basil, parsley, and scallions in a food processor and pulse until finely chopped. Add the anchovies and cheese and pulse until the mixture is a thick paste. Add the mayonnaise and puree until smooth; season with pepper to taste.

To serve, brush the surface of each hot corn cob with a light coating of the dressing and sprinkle a little more cheese over the top.

chili-roasted eggplant SERVES 4

I used to have a vegetable garden (key words: *used to*), and I had an abundance
of eggplant. It gave me anxiety. I made baba ghanoush like it was going out of style.
I eventually decided that, unlike most people who have vegetable gardens because
it's peaceful and relaxing, I was just getting wound up that as a single person I
couldn't eat all of the vegetables I was growing and I couldn't give them away fast
enough. There's a farm stand five minutes up the road, so I've decided I'll stick to
buying my vegetables there. However, I came up with some pretty good vegetable
recipes during that time that I still make today, and chili-roasted eggplant is one of
them. It is important to add the chili oil in batches, as eggplant soaks up oil like a
sponge. If you do it all at once, it won't be evenly distributed.

3	tablespoons extra-virgin olive oil, plus more for the pan
½	teaspoon chili powder
¼	teaspoon ground cumin
¼	teaspoon garlic powder
1	large globe eggplant, cut into 1-inch (2.5-cm) cubes
	Salt and freshly ground black pepper
½	lime
	Small handful of fresh mint leaves, torn
	Red chile flakes (optional)

Preheat the oven to 425°F (220°C). Lightly
oil a baking sheet.

In a small bowl, whisk the oil, chili powder,
cumin, and garlic powder together until
combined. Put the eggplant cubes in a large
mixing bowl and drizzle one third of the oil
mixture evenly over it. Toss the eggplant
to coat. Drizzle another third of the oil
over the eggplant and toss; repeat with the
remaining oil. Spread the eggplant out in an
even single layer on the baking sheet and
season it well with salt and pepper. Roast
until golden brown and soft, tossing the
eggplant with a spatula several times, about
25 minutes.

Transfer the eggplant to a serving bowl and
squeeze the lime over the top. Scatter the
torn mint over the top and garnish with a
sprinkle of chile flakes, if using. Serve hot.

BABY
EGG PLANT.
Fairy Tale
$6.90 b.

summer is best served

with a bottle of rosé

As a rule, when I'm cooking a big meal for a dinner party, I do either assembly-only hors d'oeuvres or desserts. I'm not a big baker, and generally you won't see me making beautiful cakes—except maybe my great-grandmother's Angel Food Cake (see page 191). I just don't have the patience, especially in the summer. I want yummy, simple desserts with a bit of whimsy that make me feel like a kid again.

To me, there's absolutely no better sweet treat than the humble s'more. I have so many childhood memories of building a bonfire with my cousins and roasting marshmallows. I like mine to be burnt beyond recognition then sandwiched between the graham crackers with a cheap piece of chocolate. These days, we will go out to the beach and do the same thing . . . it takes me right back.

strawberry brownie cake SERVES 8-10

I am a notorious doctorer of brownie mixes. Every year when strawberries came into season, my grandma would make a strawberry shortcake, and I have followed her tradition. Then I got to thinking . . . I love chocolate, I love strawberries, and I especially love chocolate and strawberries, so why not do a chocolate shortcake? And why not just use a brownie mix? This is so good and ridiculously simple to make and people go c-r-a-z-y for it.

2   boxes brownie mix

4   large eggs

2/3   cup (165 ml) canola oil

1   cup (240 ml) sour cream

1   cup (240 ml) prepared whipped cream (I have been known to use Cool Whip on occasion)

1   pint (335 g) strawberries, hulled and sliced

Preheat the oven to the temperature indicated on the brownie mix box. Spray two 8-inch (20-cm) round cake pans with nonstick cooking spray.

Using an electric mixer, combine the brownie mix, eggs, ¼ cup (60 ml) water, and the oil. Divide the batter between the prepared pans and bake according to the box instructions. Let cool on wire racks, then turn out of the pans. Put one brownie on a serving platter for the bottom layer.

Fold the sour cream into the whipped cream. Spread the brownie with about half of the whipped cream mixture and half of the berries. Place the second brownie layer on top. Add a scoop of the whipped cream mixture and a few berries. Slice and serve with the remaining berries and whipped cream mixture.

great-grandmother pearl's angel food cake with peaches and cream SERVES 8-10

My great-grandmother Pearl was famous for her angel food cake. She would enter baking contests with this recipe and always took home the blue ribbon. Among her bounty of prizes? A KitchenAid stand mixer (which came in very handy for this recipe, considering she used to beat the egg whites by hand) and a new stove! Not to mention a mighty fine sash and a ribbon proclaiming her the queen of cakes.

2	cups (480 ml) egg whites (from about 16 large eggs)
2	teaspoons cream of tartar
½	teaspoon salt
3	cups (600 g) sugar
2	cups (280 g) cake flour
1	teaspoon pure vanilla extract
1	teaspoon almond extract
5	peaches, cut into thin wedges
	Lightly sweetened whipped cream

Preheat the oven to 325°F (165°C).

In a standing electric mixer, beat the egg whites at medium speed until foamy. Add the cream of tartar and salt and beat until stiff peaks form. Beat in 2 ½ cups (500 g) of the sugar, a few tablespoons at a time, until smooth and glossy, about 4 minutes.

Transfer the egg whites to a large, wide bowl. Using a fine sieve, gradually sift the flour over the egg whites, gently folding in the flour with a spatula. Fold in the vanilla and almond extracts.

Scrape the batter into a 10-inch (25-cm) angel food cake pan. Using a table knife, slice through the cake batter several times to release any large air bubbles. Tap the cake pan once or twice on a flat surface. Bake in the center of the oven for 20 minutes. Increase the oven temperature to 350°F (175°C) and bake for about 35 minutes longer, until a toothpick inserted in the center comes out clean. Invert the pan onto the neck of a wine bottle and let cool completely.

Meanwhile, in a large bowl, toss the peaches with the remaining ½ cup (100 g) sugar and refrigerate, stirring occasionally, until juicy, at least 1 hour, or up to 4 hours.

To loosen the cake, run a thin-bladed knife around the side and tube of the pan. Unmold the cake and transfer to a platter. Cut the cake into wedges and serve with the peaches and whipped cream.

raspberry rosé gelatin SERVES 8

In the warm-weather months, I buy rosé by the case and we drink it like grown-up Kool-Aid. If you have leftover rosé, use it to make this gelatin, or buy an inexpensive (but still drinkable!) bottle. This is a really easy and elegant dessert, plus it is very light, so if dinner is on the heavy side this is the perfect call to finish off the meal.

2	cups (480 ml) boiling water
¾	cup (150 g) sugar
1	ounce (28 g) unflavored gelatin (such as Knox)
2	cups (480 ml) rosé wine
1	cup (125 g) raspberries
	Crème fraîche
	Edible flowers

In a large bowl, combine the boiling water, sugar, and gelatin. Whisk until the sugar and gelatin dissolve. Let cool to room temperature. Add the wine and whisk until combined.

For individual gelatins: Place 8 small ramekins or gelatin molds on a rimmed baking sheet. Place a couple of raspberries in each ramekin. Pour the wine mixture into the ramekins. Refrigerate until firm, about 4 hours.

For one large gelatin: Line a large bowl with plastic wrap and pour all of the wine mixture into the bowl. Refrigerate until firm, about 6 hours.

To loosen the gelatin from the molds, dip in shallow hot water for a few seconds. Turn out onto a serving plate. Garnish each serving with a dollop of crème fraîche and a few edible flowers and serve cold.

s'mores brownies SERVES 12

Okay, so who doesn't love s'mores? Now you don't have to have a campfire to have the same enjoyment factor. (Did that just sound like an infomercial tag line? For $19.99 you can have s'mores any time you like . . . if you call right now!) I'm typically a proponent of making things from scratch, but when it comes to brownies, I go for the box and dress 'em up a little bit. If you want to get really decadent, you can swirl a little melted peanut butter into the batter as well.

1 ½   cups (125 g) crushed graham crackers

3   tablespoons sugar

4   tablespoons (½ stick/55 g) unsalted butter, melted

1   box brownie mix

3   cups (165 g) regular marshmallows

Preheat the oven to 325°F (165°C). Lightly coat an 8-inch (20-cm) square baking dish with nonstick cooking spray.

In a medium bowl, combine the graham cracker crumbs and sugar. Stir in the melted butter. Transfer the crumb mixture to the prepared baking dish and use a measuring cup to press the crumbs evenly over the bottom of the pan. Bake until golden brown, 10 to 15 minutes.

Meanwhile, prepare the brownie mix according to the package instructions (make sure to use a broiler-safe pan). Pour the batter over the prepared crust. Bake until a toothpick comes out mostly clean, about 40 minutes. Remove from the oven and position the oven rack under the broiler.

Preheat the broiler.

Top the brownie with the marshmallows and put under the broiler for 1 to 2 minutes with the oven door open a few inches, until the marshmallows are toasted. Watch closely to prevent burning. Let cool completely on a wire rack. Cut into squares and serve.

kiwi blueberry pavlova SERVES 8

Pavlova is one of my go-to desserts when I'm trying to impress. It is so easy—wait, let me emphasize that sentiment: *so easy*. If you're unfamiliar with pavlova, it is basically a large meringue with whipped cream and fruit, and it is very popular in Australia. Any fruit can be used; sometimes I'll do peaches or strawberries, whatever looks best at the market. Prepare yourself for the oooohhhs and ahhhhhs you'll receive!

6	large egg whites
1 ½	cups (180 g) confectioners' sugar
3	tablespoons cornstarch
1	tablespoon white vinegar
1	cup (240 ml) heavy cream
1	teaspoon vanilla extract
3	kiwi fruit, peeled and diced
1	pint (335 g) blueberries

Preheat the oven to 300°F (150°C). Line a baking sheet with parchment paper.

In a standing electric mixer, beat the egg whites on high speed for 1 minute. With the mixer still on, slowly add 1 cup (120 g) of the confectioners' sugar. Continue to beat on high until glossy and stiff peaks form, about 4 more minutes. Turn off the mixer and use a spatula to gently fold in the cornstarch and vinegar.

Scoop the meringue into the center of the prepared baking sheet and spread it into a 9-inch (23-cm) circle. Put in the oven and lower the oven temperature to 250°F (120°C). Bake for 1 hour. Turn off the oven, but do not open the door, and let the meringue cool completely, about 1 hour.

Using an electric mixer, whip the cream with the remaining ½ cup (60 g) confectioners' sugar until soft peaks form; do not overbeat. Stir in the vanilla.

In a bowl, combine the kiwi and blueberries.

Place the meringue disk on a serving plate and spread with whipped cream. Spoon the kiwi and blueberries into the center of the meringue, leaving a border around the edge. Serve immediately.

pecan ice cream balls with fudge sauce SERVES 6-8

Remember the drumsticks you used to get as a kid from the ice cream truck? These pecan ice cream balls with fudge sauce are kind of like a grown-up version of those. They're super easy to make and great to serve at a dinner party because you can make them ahead of time and just give the fudge sauce a quick reheat at the last minute. And you can do as I do and make a few extra to have around for TV watching.

2 ½ pints (1.2 kg) vanilla ice cream

2 cups (6 ounces/170 g) pecan halves

1 (12-ounce/340-g) bag semi-sweet chocolate chips, or 12 ounces (340 g) semisweet chocolate cut into chunks

1 (14-ounce/396-g) can sweetened condensed milk

4 tablespoons (½ stick/55 g) unsalted butter

1 teaspoon pure vanilla extract

Preheat the oven to 350°F (175°C). Put the ice cream in the refrigerator until just softened, about 15 minutes. Line a baking sheet with waxed paper and transfer it to the freezer.

Spread the pecans on a baking sheet and toast until fragrant and browned, about 8 minutes; transfer to a food processor and let cool completely. Coarsely chop the nuts and transfer to a pie plate.

Using an ice cream scoop, scoop ice cream onto the pecans and roll into a ball, pressing lightly to help the nuts adhere. Transfer the ice cream ball to the prepared baking sheet in the freezer. Repeat with the remaining ice cream and pecans. Freeze the ice cream balls for at least 3 hours before serving.

Meanwhile, in a medium saucepan, combine the chocolate chips, condensed milk, and butter and cook over low heat, stirring, until the chocolate is completely melted and the sauce is smooth. Remove from the heat and stir in the vanilla. Transfer the sauce to a pitcher.

Serve the ice cream in bowls or sundae cups and drizzle with the warm sauce.

peach blueberry skillet cobbler SERVES 8

If you think you can't bake, this recipe is for you: It is beyond easy and is seriously delicious. I think it looks really cool in the iron skillet for serving, but if you don't have one (you should probably buy one because they're pretty awesome), you can bake this in a regular baking dish. In any case, this is great served with vanilla ice cream.

4	cups (615 g) sliced peaches (I leave the peels on, but it's up to you)
1	cup (150 g) blueberries
1½	teaspoons fresh lemon juice
1	cup (200 g) sugar
1	cup (130 g) all-purpose flour
1	teaspoon baking powder
1	teaspoon salt
½	cup (120 ml) milk
4	tablespoons (½ stick/55 g) unsalted butter, melted
1	tablespoon cornstarch
½	cup (120 ml) boiling water

Preheat the oven to 325°F (165°C).

Put the peaches and blueberries in a 10-inch (25-cm) cast-iron skillet and toss with lemon juice.

In a medium bowl, whisk together ¾ cup (150 g) of the sugar, the flour, baking powder, and salt. Add the milk and melted butter and mix with a rubber spatula until the ingredients are just blended. Pour the batter evenly over the peaches and blueberries.

In a small bowl, whisk together the remaining ¼ cup (50 g) sugar and the cornstarch. Sprinkle the sugar mixture across the batter, then pour the boiling water evenly over the top of the batter, moistening all of the sugar mixture. Bake for 55 to 60 minutes, until golden brown and bubbling. Remove from the oven and place on a cooling rack to set for 10 minutes. Serve warm.

light lemony berry cheesecake

SERVES 8

My mom is a very health-conscious cook, sometimes to a fault. (Sorry, Mom.) This cheesecake happens to be one of her healthy dishes that's also a standout in the taste department. I'll bet no one you serve this to would ever know it's not a straight-up full-fat cheesecake.

Nonstick cooking spray

¾ cup (60 g) whole-wheat graham cracker crumbs (sometimes I use amaretti cookies as a substitute)

2 cups (480 ml) light cottage cheese

1 (8-ounce/225-g) package light cream cheese

3 large eggs

¾ cup (150 g) sugar, plus a little more for the berries

1 tablespoon grated lemon zest

¼ cup (60 ml) fresh lemon juice

2 tablespoons all-purpose flour

1 teaspoon vanilla extract

Sliced strawberries, raspberries, and blackberries

Preheat the oven to 375°F (190°C). Spray a 9-inch (23-cm) springform pan with cooking spray.

Use a measuring cup to gently press the graham cracker crumbs into the bottom of the prepared pan. Spray the crust with cooking spray. The crust will not be very thick.

In a blender, combine the cottage cheese, cream cheese, eggs, sugar, lemon zest, lemon juice, flour, and vanilla and blend until smooth. Pour into the crust and bake for 40 minutes. Let cool completely. Chill in the refrigerator for at least 4 hours, or up to overnight.

Toss the berries with a pinch of sugar. Serve the cheesecake cold, topping each slice with some of the berries.

apricots with almond crumble

SERVES 4

A "crumble" is one of my favorite simple summer desserts. This recipe can be used with any stone fruit, or even with apples substituted in the fall.

1	tablespoon unsalted butter, at room temperature, plus more for the baking dish
4	apricots, peeled, halved through the stem, and pitted
2	tablespoons finely chopped almonds
2	tablespoons rolled oats
2	tablespoons light brown sugar
¼	teaspoon ground cinnamon

Preheat the oven to 400°F (205°C). Grease a small shallow baking dish with butter and place the apricot halves, cut side up, in the dish.

In a small bowl, mix together the butter, almonds, oats, brown sugar, and cinnamon until it forms small clumps. Sprinkle the almond mixture over the cut apricot halves, covering them completely. Bake until golden brown, about 20 minutes.

Cool for at least 5 minutes before serving.

apricot tarts SERVES 6

I like to make desserts that don't take too much time and can basically just be assembled, especially if I'm already cooking a big meal. These apricot tarts are simple as can be. Plus, they look so sweet and adorable and they let the fruit really shine in the brilliance of its seasonality.

1   sheet frozen puff pastry, thawed (I like Dufour pastry)

2   tablespoons light brown sugar

6   apricots, halved lengthwise, pits removed

2   tablespoons unsalted butter, diced

    Whipped cream

    Toasted sliced almonds

Preheat the oven to 400°F (205°C). Line a baking sheet with parchment paper.

Unfold the puff pastry on a work surface and press it with the palm of your hand to flatten it. Cut the sheet into six equal-size rectangles, about 3 by 4 ¾ inches (7.5 by 12 cm), and transfer them to the baking sheet.

Evenly sprinkle 1 tablespoon of the brown sugar over the surface of the rectangles. Set two apricot halves, cut side up, on each rectangle and sprinkle the remaining brown sugar evenly over each tart. Top each apricot with a piece of butter.

Bake until the tarts are golden brown around the edges and puffy, about 20 minutes. Let cool to room temperature and serve with a dollop of whipped cream and some almonds sprinkled over the top.

corn ice
pops

minty
watermelon
lemonade
pops

minty watermelon lemonade pops

MAKES 10 ICE POPS

These pops are even more refreshing than they sound. When it's super hot outside, they'll cool you right off. I like these for a pool party, especially after serving my West Virginia hot dogs (see page 154).

4   cups (600 g) cubed watermelon, seeds removed

1   cup (240 ml) lemonade

¼   cup (60 ml) simple syrup

¼   cup (10 g) fresh mint leaves

Combine all the ingredients in a blender and blend until smooth. Pour into ice pop molds and freeze until firm.

campari-citrus ice pops MAKES 10 ICE POPS

These pops are for grown-ups only! The color is so vibrant. They are perfect for dessert, but also really fun for something different at cocktail hour.

3   cups (700 ml) fresh orange juice

1   cup (240 ml) Campari

1   cup (240 ml) simple syrup

Juice of 1 lemon

In a pitcher, combine all the ingredients. Pour into ice pop molds and freeze until firm.

corn ice pops MAKES 10 ICE POPS

You know when you have a sweet corn cereal and you eat all the cereal out of the bowl and then drink the milk? That cereal-soaked milk is what these pops taste like. This might sound kind of bizarre, but trust me, these pops are *ah-may-zing*. Like, you-can't-stop-eating-them good (and honestly, I don't feel guilty about eating these).

4   ears sweet corn, kernels cut off the cobs, cobs reserved

2   cups (480 ml) whole milk

1   cup (240 ml) plain Greek yogurt

½   cup (120 ml) agave syrup

    Pinch of sea salt

½   teaspoon pure vanilla extract

In a medium saucepan, heat the milk, corn kernels, and corncobs over medium heat until the milk is bubbly, then reduce the heat and simmer for 20 minutes. Remove from the heat and let cool for about 10 minutes. Discard the cobs. Use a slotted spoon to remove about 1 cup (145 g) of the kernels and set them aside.

In a blender, combine the corn and milk mixture, the yogurt, agave syrup, salt, and vanilla and blend until smooth. Add the reserved corn and pulse once on low speed. Pour into ice pop molds and freeze until firm.

cherry chocolate chunk cookie and cherry ice cream sandwiches

MAKES 12 ICE CREAM SANDWICHES

Years ago, Gwyneth Paltrow invited me to dinner at her home in Amagansett. What does one bring to Gwyneth Paltrow's house for a hostess gift? A candle or a bottle of wine just didn't seem right; when in doubt, chocolate chip cookies. Well, I was out of chocolate chips, and it was too late to go to the grocery store. In my pantry I found a chocolate bar and broke it into pieces. It didn't seem like enough, so I threw in some dried cherries. Gwyneth cooked an awesome meal that night—I remember she made these perfectly grilled whole chickens and this lobster Cobb salad with duck bacon that was just delicious. When it was time for dessert, the cookies were a hit! She even asked me for the recipe to post on her website Goop. Here I've taken those same cookies up a notch by adding cocoa and turning them into ice cream sandwiches with cherry ice cream. Make some homemade ice cream or just buy it!

2 cups (255 g) all-purpose flour

1/3 cup (30 g) unsweetened cocoa powder

3/4 teaspoon salt

1/2 teaspoon baking powder

1/2 teaspoon baking soda

1/2 cup (1 stick/115 g) unsalted butter, at room temperature

2/3 cup (150 g) packed dark brown sugar

2/3 cup (130 g) granulated sugar

1 teaspoon pure vanilla extract

2 large eggs, at room temperature

8 ounces (225 g) dark chocolate (at least 60% cocoa content), chopped

1 cup (170 g) dried cherries, coarsely chopped

2 pints (960 ml) cherry ice cream

Preheat the oven to 375°F (190°C). Line two baking sheets with parchment paper.

Sift the flour, cocoa powder, salt, baking powder, and baking soda into a large bowl. In the bowl of a standing electric mixer fitted with the paddle attachment (or using a handheld mixer), beat the butter, brown sugar, granulated sugar, and vanilla on high speed until light and fluffy, about 3 minutes. Reduce the mixer's speed to medium and add the eggs, one at a time, beating until incorporated, about 1 minute.

On low speed, gradually add the dry ingredients and mix until just combined. Remove the bowl from the mixer and using a rubber spatula, mix in the chocolate and cherries by hand. Scoop by 2-heaping-tablespoonful amounts (or use a 2-inch/5-cm diameter ice cream scoop) onto the prepared baking sheets. Moisten the heel of your hand and fingers with water and flatten the cookies until they are perfectly round, about ¼ inch (6 mm) thick and 3 inches (7.5 cm) in diameter. Place 6 cookies on each baking sheet, spacing them 1 inch (2.5 cm) apart. Bake the cookies until they are set in the center, 10 to 12 minutes, rotating the pans halfway through baking. Transfer the baking sheets to cooling racks to set for 5 minutes. Leave the warm cookies on the parchment paper and carefully slide them with the parchment off the baking sheet and onto cooling racks to cool completely. Let the baking sheets come to room temperature, line them with parchment paper again, and repeat the steps for the second batch of cookies.

When all the cookies have cooled completely, you are ready to assemble the sandwiches. Allow the ice cream to soften until it is easy to scoop. Spoon ¼ cup (60 ml) onto half of the chocolate cookies and top with the remaining cookies to create sandwiches. Freeze on a baking sheet for 30 minutes. Serve immediately, or wrap individually in plastic wrap and store in a freezer bag to serve later. The ice cream sandwiches will keep frozen for up to 2 months.

limoncello ginger tiramisù SERVES 8

When I go to an Italian restaurant, I usually order tiramisù for dessert if it's on the menu. I love it as a summer dessert since it's so light. I got to thinking, why not play around with the traditional recipe and do something a little different? I used limoncello, in keeping with the Italian vibe, and added a little ginger for some zing. It's so light and refreshing, a perfect end to a summer meal on a hot night. I like making this when I serve grilled chicken Parmesan (see page 127). The best part is that you can make it completely in advance.

½ cup (100 g) sugar

1 6-inch (15 cm) piece of ginger, finely chopped

⅓ cup (75 ml) limoncello (Italian lemon liqueur)

8 ounces (225 g) mascarpone cheese, at room temperature

1 (10-ounce/284-g) jar lemon curd

1 cup (240 ml) heavy cream, whipped to medium peaks

1 (7-ounce/200-g) package crisp ladyfingers (Savoiardi; 24 total)

In a small saucepan, bring the sugar, ½ cup (120 ml) water, and the ginger to a boil. Remove from the heat and let stand until completely cool. Strain the syrup through a fine-mesh sieve into a shallow dish, pressing on the ginger to remove as much liquid as possible. Add the limoncello to the syrup and stir to combine.

Put the mascarpone in a medium bowl and fold it a few times with a large rubber spatula to loosen it. Stir the lemon curd and add it to the mascarpone. Using the spatula, gently fold the curd into the mascarpone until just combined and no streaks of white remain. Add one third of the whipped cream and fold lightly to combine; add the remaining whipped cream and fold gently, turning the bowl, until the mixture is homogenous and no streaks of white remain.

Briefly dipping both sides of half of the ladyfingers into the ginger-limoncello mixture (to moisten the cookies but not soak them), line the bottom of an 8-inch (20-cm) square baking dish or cake pan with 6 ladyfingers in 2 rows, trimming the edges to fit if necessary. (Place the trimmings in a small bowl and steal a spoonful of the filling to dollop over them and enjoy as a private little cook's treat.) Pour half of the lemon cream mixture into the pan, and with a small offset spatula, spread the filling evenly over the ladyfingers. Repeat with the remaining ladyfingers, trimming them exactly like the first layer; you may need to flip them over in the syrup in order to dip both sides once the syrup begins to run out. Spread the remaining cream over the top. Lightly cover the dish with plastic wrap and refrigerate for at least 4 hours and preferably overnight.

To serve, slice with a warm, dry knife.

acknowledgments

I owe a very big thank you to my team at Abrams in making the dream of this cookbook a reality. From our first meeting, I knew I wanted to work with these people, and I wanted to hang out with them, too! Holly Dolce is an incredible editor and Deb Wood a killer art director. These are two women with vision! They led me to Lucy Schaeffer, photographer extraordinaire. Lucy is an incredible talent who captured the essence of summer in every shot (and she's a trouper—on our last day of shooting, she worked through the pain of a blown-out Achilles from a street hockey injury the day before). My recipes were tested by one of the kindest, most knowledgeable men in food, Wes Martin. The recipes were styled to perfection by Paul Lowe and Mariana Velasquez and the lovely props were by Leslie Siegel. Thank you to Elizabeth Stone, Sarah Massey, Emily Albarillo, Liana Krissoff, Leda Scheintaub, Patricia Austin, Sarah Schuffle, and Denise LaCongo.

My Food Network family has been such an incredible source of support, and I owe a great deal of gratitude to everyone there, especially Brooke Johnson, Bob Tuschman, Allison Page, Irika Slavin, Susie Fogelson, Amanda Melnick, Karen Berrios, and Jill Novatt. Working on *The Kitchen* is fulfilling in so many ways and our viewers helped shape this book as well. Through their tweets and Instagram feedback, I was given a better idea of the kinds of recipes people want to make. Beth Burke and Blake Swerdloff produce a great show, and I am so grateful to be a part of it.

My publicity group at Sunshine Sachs—Shawn Sachs, Pamela Spiegel, and Crystal Wang—does a terrific job and I am so happy to work with them.

I'd also like to thank my "guinea pigs" for tasting all of my creations while I was recipe testing and providing their honest input and opinions: Keith Bloomfield, Mark Mullett, Beth Stern, Nick Murtha, Marcy Blum, Ben and Megan Shaoul, Gretta Monahan, Ricky Goldin, Suzanne Lyon, Bobby Flay, and my mom.

Thank you to the farmers of land and sea in the Hamptons, especially the Green Thumb.

My grandma is my biggest culinary inspiration, so everything always goes back to her. Thanks, Granny. Love you.

Katie Lee is a co-host of Food Network's *The Kitchen*. She has written two other cookbooks and a novel. Outside of her culinary and literary adventures, she enjoys surfing, traveling, and playing with her pug, Fionula. She resides in the Hamptons and New York City.

Editor: Holly Dolce
Designer: Deb Wood
Production Manager: Denise LaCongo

Library of Congress Control Number: 2017949645

ISBN: 978-1-4197-3105-1

The text of this book was composed in Neutra,
with handwritten type by Deb Wood.

Printed and bound in China
10 9 8 7 6 5 4 3 2 1

Abrams books are available at special discounts when
purchased in quantity for premiums and promotions as
well as fundraising or educational use. Special editions
can also be created to specification. For details, contact
specialsales@abramsbooks.com or the address below.

ABRAMS The Art of Books
195 Broadway, New York, NY 10007
abramsbooks.com